Resisting Rape Culture

Resisting Rape Culture tackles controversial and harrowing rape myths prevalent in rape culture: namely, that sex workers do not get raped, and that they are deserving victims of sexual violence. Commonly, sociocultural discourses depict sex workers as morally deficient and promiscuous, having sex with multiple clients in exchange for payment. Consequently, they are often considered deserving of rape, sexual assault and other forms of abuse, or as people who should expect to receive such treatment. In a way, the Hebrew Bible contributes to such stigmatization of and discrimination against sex workers, given first, its authority and second, its negative portrayals of prostitutes as outsiders.

This cutting-edge book describes the rape culture in Hong Kong, focusing on how Hong Kong Christians interpret the Bible concerning prostitutes, and in turn how this affects the treatment of sex workers. Arguably, when interpretations malign the prostitutes in the Bible, and do not critique how the Bible portrays these women, we promote the stigmatization of sex workers and, in doing so, normalise and trivialise sexual discrimination, abuse and violence, ultimately promoting rape culture.

Nancy Nam Hoon Tan is an independent scholar based in Singapore. Until January 2020, she was the Associate Professor in Hebrew Bible at Divinity School of Chung Chi College, the Chinese University of Hong Kong.

Rape Culture, Religion and the Bible
Series Editors:

Katie Edwards
University of Sheffield, UK

Caroline Anne Blyth
University of Auckland, New Zealand

Johanna Stiebert
University of Leeds, UK

Rape Myths, the Bible and #MeToo
Johanna Stiebert

Telling Terror in Judges 19
Rape and Reparation for the Levite's wife
Helen Paynter

Resisting Rape Culture
The Hebrew Bible and Hong Kong Sex Workers
Nany Nam Hoon Tan

The Bible and Sexual Violence Against Men
Chris Greenough

For more information about this series, please visit: https://www.routledge.com/Rape-Culture-Religion-and-the-Bible/book-series/RCRB

Resisting Rape Culture
The Hebrew Bible and
Hong Kong Sex Workers

Nancy Nam Hoon Tan

LONDON AND NEW YORK

First published 2021
by Routledge
2 Park Square, Milton Park, Abingdon, Oxon OX14 4RN

and by Routledge
605 Third Avenue, New York, NY 10017

First issued in paperback 2022

Routledge is an imprint of the Taylor & Francis Group, an informa business

© 2021 Nancy Nam Hoon Tan

The right of Nancy Nam Hoon Tan to be identified as author of this work has been asserted by her in accordance with sections 77 and 78 of the Copyright, Designs and Patents Act 1988.

All rights reserved. No part of this book may be reprinted or reproduced or utilised in any form or by any electronic, mechanical, or other means, now known or hereafter invented, including photocopying and recording, or in any information storage or retrieval system, without permission in writing from the publishers.

Trademark notice: Product or corporate names may be trademarks or registered trademarks, and are used only for identification and explanation without intent to infringe.

Publisher's Note
The publisher has gone to great lengths to ensure the quality of this reprint but points out that some imperfections in the original copies may be apparent.

British Library Cataloguing-in-Publication Data
A catalogue record for this book is available from the British Library

Library of Congress Cataloging-in-Publication Data
Names: Tan, Nancy Nam Hoon, author.
Title: Resisting rape culture: the Hebrew Bible and Hong Kong sex workers / Nancy Nam Hoon Tan.
Description: Abingdon, Oxon; New York, NY: Routledge, 2021. | Series: Rape culture, religion and the bible | Includes bibliographical references and index. |
Identifiers: LCCN 2020015746 | ISBN 9780367353834 (hbk) | ISBN 9780429331121 (ebk) | ISBN 9780367544980 (pbk)
Subjects: LCSH: Rape in the Bible. | Bible. Genesis, XXXVIII–Criticism, interpretation, etc.–China–Hong Kong. | Bible. Hosea, I-III–Criticism, interpretation, etc.–China–Hong Kong. | Sex workers–China–Hong Kong.
Classification: LCC BS1199.R27 T36 2021 | DDC 221.8/30674–dc23
LC record available at https://lccn.loc.gov/2020015746

ISBN: 978–0–367–54498–0 (pbk)
ISBN: 978–0–367–35383–4 (hbk)
ISBN: 978–0–429–33112–1 (ebk)

DOI: 10.4324/9780429331121

Typeset in Bembo
by Deanta Global Publishing Services, Chennai, India

Contents

Acknowledgements viii

1 Introduction 1
   1.1 *Purpose of the book* 3
   1.2 *Standpoint theory* 5
   1.3 *The three biblical stories and the reading exercises* 8
   1.4 *Synopsis* 9
   Notes 10

2 Rape culture and sex work in Hong Kong 13
   2.1 *Rape laws in Hong Kong* 13
   2.2 *Rape statistics in Hong Kong* 15
   2.3 *Rape culture and resistance in Hong Kong* 16
   2.4 *Sex work in Hong Kong* 21
      2.4.1 *General background information about sex workers* 21
      2.4.2 *Advocacy for sex workers in Hong Kong* 22
      2.4.3 *Hong Kong laws governing sex work* 24
      2.4.4 *Consequences of the laws regulating sex work* 25
      2.4.5 *Section summary* 26
   Notes 27

3 Sex workers read Tamar 31
   3.1 *The story in Genesis 38* 31
   3.2 *Hong Kong Christian interpretations* 32
      3.2.1 *Tamar is to return home in Gen 38:11* 33
      3.2.2 *Tamar's actions in 38:14 and her conception in 38:18* 34
      3.2.3 *Hirah's search for the* qdsh *in Gen 38:20–23* 35

3.2.4 Judah sentences Tamar to death in Gen 38:24–25 35
3.2.5 General summary of Hong Kong Christian interpretations 36
3.3 The sex workers' standpoint 37
3.3.1 Gen 38:9 is a rape text 38
3.3.2 Gen 38:14 is the climax of the story 40
3.3.2.1 What Tamar sees 40
3.3.2.2 What Tamar does to seduce Judah 42
3.3.3 Hirah's use of qdsh 46
3.3.3.1 qdsh means an outsider 46
3.3.3.2 Tamar is neither a qdsh nor a prostitute 48
3.4 Chapter summary 48
Notes 49

4 Sex workers read the story of the two prostitutes and King Solomon 53
4.1 The story of the two prostitutes and King Solomon 55
4.2 Hong Kong Christian interpretations 56
4.2.1 Purpose of the story 56
4.2.2 Interpretations concerning the prostitutes 57
4.3 Sex workers' standpoints 57
4.3.1 Sympathy for the two prostitutes 57
4.3.2 Violence disguised as wisdom 58
4.3.3 The biblical author marginalises the prostitutes and their children 62
4.4 Chapter summary 64
Notes 65

5 Sex workers read Gomer and the female prostitution figures in Hosea 1–3 68
5.1 Gomer and the female prostitution figures in Hosea 1–3 69
5.2 Hong Kong Christian interpretations 70
5.2.1 Prostitute, wife and mother 70
5.2.2 Justifications for punishment 72
5.3 Sex workers' standpoints 74
5.3.1 The problem of Hosea/YHWH condoning rape culture 75
5.3.2 The victimization of Gomer and the female prostitution figures 76

    5.3.3 The problem of the female prostitution metaphors 79
  5.4 Chapter summary 83
  Notes 84

6 Summary and conclusion   86

  Selected bibliography   91
  Subjects and authors index   94
  Biblical texts index   97

Acknowledgements

First and foremost, to all the "sisters" at Jei Jei Jai Association, and their co-ordinator (2008–18), Sherry Lai Kwan, Hui, I owe my deepest gratitude. When I was at the lowest point of my life, they taught me what it meant to live life courageously despite the most trying circumstances. This book could not have been accomplished without them and it is meaningless if it were not for them. Hence, it is with deep gratitude that this work is specially dedicated to all the "sisters" at Jei Jei Jai Association and Hong Kong. I sincerely hope that with this book, readers may join me to appreciate and celebrate the wit, wisdom, intelligence and ingenuity these "sisters" have demonstrated in their interpretations of the biblical stories.

The second group of people to whom I owe my gratitude are the colleagues in the UK whom I have gotten to know during the course of my academic career. Heather A. McKay, who, ever since we met, has not ceased to encourage, motivate and give me emotional and moral support. She proofread this manuscript and taught me many things through the process. Johanna Stiebert is another endearing colleague who is most generous, selfless and kind especially towards Asian and non-Western people—looking out for ways to promote their academic reputation and career in the Western world. I want to thank her for initiating the idea of this book from the start, and helping and cheering me on throughout the process until its publication.

The third group are my colleagues—the teaching staff, and above all, the lovely team of administrative and pastoral staff, along with the vibrant students of Divinity School of Chung Chi College, the Chinese University of Hong Kong (CUHK). It is with deep gratitude to the institution that I was able to enjoy and practice academic freedom and, through interaction with my esteemed colleagues, mature in my research in the Hebrew Bible especially on issues related to justice and social responsibility.

Acknowledgements ix

I was a campus resident of the Chung Chi College (CCC), CUHK since 2005. While I was writing this book in November 2019, the ongoing Hong Kong protests took a dramatic turn of events. In the course of describing the events that happened to CUHK below, I also want to acknowledge the same traumatic experiences that Hong Kong Polytechnic University underwent. Comparatively speaking, their ordeal went on for 12 days and the intensity of the invasion and destruction far exceeded that of CUHK.

The notion of ignored "consent" in rape became real for the campus residents of CUHK when the Hong Kong Riot Police intruded into the campus grounds for the first time on 11 November 2019. The police wanted to stop protesters on CUHK campus from throwing objects onto the train tracks that would obstruct the operation of the northern line of the Mass Transit Railway. The university's management team attempted to negotiate and mediate with the police to not enter the campus but the latter ignored the pleas, entering the university through a bridge from the Tolo Highway. On that day, the police fired over a hundred canisters of tear gas and rubber bullets. The protesters reacted to the police intrusion, and fortified the whole campus, setting up barricades to all the main entrances. On 12 November, the Hong Kong Riot Police suddenly opened fire at the students and the Vice-Chancellor while the latter was walking back and forth in the process of negotiating a truce between the two opposing parties. At that time, nearly 200 or more CCC alumni were on campus for they had returned to support the students and staff in residence, in the hope that the police would retreat. Unfortunately, their efforts were to no avail. Over 1,567 canisters of tear gas, 1,312 rubber bullets, 380 bean-bag rounds and 126 sponge grenades were fired. A thick cloud of tear gas covered CCC grounds. All of the residents and the alumni who were on CCC campus grounds were poisoned by the tear gas. Many were also injured while trying to flee the attack. The protesters were enraged and in the days following, further destruction was done to the environment and facilities on campus. The protesters set up more barricades which closed all access to CUHK including Tai Po Road and the Tolo Highway. The university was completely shut down. This led to a series of evacuations of the students from the hostels, and finally the mass exile of all campus residents on 15 November—a day we will never forget. We had to climb up slopes, track on narrow roads and paths, and cross the barricades with our luggage—which took 40 minutes or more—in order to get out of the campus vicinity. At that time, we did not know when we might or could return to our homes. Fear, confusion, feelings of loss, disappointment, indignation, anger, frustration, exasperation and many more indescribable emotions are probably the very same ones, if not in more intensity, that plague all victims of rape and other sexual offences. At least for CUHK, the whole community returned and came together to rebuild and restore the campus as soon as we were able to take control of it. But the victims of rape and other sexual offences, who continue to suffer injustice in silence, and perhaps continually build up defences to shield themselves from all negative forces, yet still find people to listen to and believe their stories, must be experiencing intolerable torture to their whole being. I hope this volume gives you, whoever you are and wherever you may be, courage to live, trust and hope.

1 Introduction

On 12 October 2017, the High Court of the Special Administrative Region of Hong Kong convicted a male shipping clerk, Mr Gary Leung, to 11 years' imprisonment for raping a sex worker and stealing HK$1600 (US$205) and her mobile phone.[1]

On 1 December 2016, Leung approached a sex worker's flat, allegedly for services. The sex worker let him in and when she turned her back to him, he pulled out a knife to threaten her. He bound her wrists and ankles and raped her. When, after this, the doorbell rang, he took off with her money and mobile phone. Her neighbour called the police after hearing the commotion and realising what had happened. Leung was caught after the police circulated a photograph of him taken from CCTV. The jury, composed of three men and four women, reached their verdict within one hour, finding Leung guilty on two counts: rape and theft. Leung persisted in his denial of both charges, claiming that there had been an agreed transaction to role-play "rape" for the agreed amount. The (female) judge rejected an appeal for a lighter sentence, because evidence from Leung's mobile phone proved that the crimes of rape and theft had been premeditated. The history of searches on Leung's phone showed that, before he committed the crimes, he had researched how to rape and rob a sex worker. After the crimes, he also searched for updated police reports on rape and theft within the victim's district. The judge justified the "harsh" sentence in terms of a "deterrent" and deemed the accused "shameless" for his actions towards the sex worker who was extremely vulnerable and trying to do her job. Throughout the court hearing, the sex worker's identity was confidential and protected. The procedure and the outcome indeed deserve praise.

On the Facebook page for a local Chinese online news service, a post reporting on this trial was met with many responses that praised the verdict and denounced Leung.[2] Comparatively speaking, about one-third of the comments, however, may be considered negative. There were comments saying that Leung deserved the sentence because of his stupidity, rather than his criminal behaviour. Moreover, there were many comments that used strongly derogatory language towards the victim. That is, some comments, while seemingly agreeing with the sentence, consistently used demeaning language for the sex worker, making judgements about her on account of her profession, as opposed to emphasising her status as a victim of violence. Several comments also questioned the severity of the sentence, not considering the judge's verdict in this particular case to constitute a "deterrent". Many responders to the report regarded the overall outcome of the investigation, as well as the verdict and its general reception, quite positively, but on scrolling through the responses from the public, positive comments such as "such crimes deserve heavy penalties" were persistently interspersed with negative ones, downplaying the seriousness of rape when the victim is a sex worker. I argue that such comments are a significant indicator that a largely unexamined rape culture continues to exist alongside more measured attitudes.

When I interviewed Ms Sherry Hui, the coordinator for the Jei Jei Jai[3] Association (hereafter JJJ), a non-governmental organization (NGO) for sex workers, I asked whether sex workers now feel safer and more confident with the judicial system. Hui replied that sex workers were happy with the outcome, but considered this particular sex worker to have been comparatively lucky. Many of the sex workers, she told me, have had similar or worse experiences of sexual violence but chose not to report them. The Hong Kong sex workers reasoned that Leung was convicted because he was an ordinary clerk. Making an example of someone like him was much easier than if a culprit were to be someone of social standing, with a more respectable career, such as an engineer, a doctor or a successful entrepreneur. Such a man, they believed, would probably not be prosecuted at all. This indicates that among sex workers, trust in the judicial system is still limited.

Before I proceed, let me explain that I take "rape culture" to refer to the social phenomenon whereby—for some people—the crime of rape is excused while victims are both blamed and stigmatised. What I have described above indicates how a significant sector of the Hong Kong public responded to reports of the trial and verdict by emphasising the culprit's stupidity and that the sentence passed on this rapist was too harsh. This shows a clear belittling of the crime of rape. Some of the attitudes suggest that Leung was stupid and careless rather than vicious and criminal; others suggest that he does not deserve such a heavy penalty. Some comments reflect that since "sex is what sex workers do", what Leung did does not constitute rape or should receive a lighter sentence. Hence, some comments jeered at Leung for having to serve a penalty over a sex worker "of all persons". This reflects the attitude that rape is excusable or pardonable in certain cases; it is not even a crime for "those and such as those". But rape *is* a grave and violent crime regardless of the social status, wealth, cognitive ability, ethnicity or profession of the perpetrator. And the effects of rape are damaging for any victim regardless of their social status, wealth, cognitive ability, ethnicity or profession. A sex worker can be and often is a victim of rape and a sex worker's trauma and rights to justice should be equally acknowledged and respected.

Particularly at issue here are two rape myths: 1) that sex workers do not get raped (i.e. sex workers get paid for sex and as long as they get paid, they can be subjected to any sexual act); and 2) that sex workers deserve to be raped because of their profession (i.e. sex workers are not entitled to the rights and privileges of others, because they are less moral and less worthy). Persons who express such opinions, explicitly or by implication, seem not to understand that in sex work, permission for, and agreement to, the kind of sex services offered are negotiated and remain paramount before, throughout and after the service. Any action compromising or violating what has been agreed and permitted infringes consent and is a crime. Unfortunately, the responses on social media indicate that rape myths continue to propagate the notions that women, and men, too, get raped because they "asked for it", by virtue of their appearance or their behaviours. And often these notions are created and determined by the perpetrator's gaze. Perpetrators can still and often do what they wish, or feel entitled to be sexually aggressive, because rape cultures continue to tolerate and even to support and facilitate such attitudes. Sex workers, in particular, suffer from such attitudes to their detriment. Sex workers, in particular, have no right to "cry rape". Those who disregard or despise sex workers and their rights do not understand what the judge was saying when she asserted the truth that sex workers are vulnerable to rape because of their profession.[4]

Rape myths are transmitters of violence and injustice and sex workers are particularly vulnerable to physical, including sexual, violence. They are also less likely than many other victims to seek out legal defence. The Hong Kong sex workers' continuing distrust in the ability of the judicial system to defend their cause in the event of rape or other sexual abuse shows that rape myths continue to hold sway. I hope this volume will make a significant contribution to confront and curb the perpetuation of such damaging falsehoods.

1.1 Purpose of the book

This book focuses on prejudice against sex workers, using well-known Bible texts about "prostitutes" (see below) and data collected with sex workers in Hong Kong. It tackles a pernicious and dangerous rape myth: namely, that women *perceived* to be promiscuous because they have multiple sexual partners, and sex workers in particular, deserve to be stigmatised, punished and even raped. I have used the word "perceived" here because it is often the case that a court of law defends an alleged perpetrator as long as doubt can be raised that the victim (called the "complainant") has behaved in a way that indicates or implies consent. If that can be proven, then an alleged perpetrator is not found to be a criminal, even when evidence against them may be strong.[5] When such a case is dismissed, the victim is left exactly as before and possibly even worse—because a court and maybe the public, too, have dismissed or condemned them, causing feelings of rejection and dejection.

As may be gauged from the case cited above, as well as from some of the public responses to this case, sex workers, by virtue of their profession, are at high risk of sexual violence. Moreover, sex workers' accounts of ill treatment are often disbelieved, they rarely seek legal defence and those who perpetrate violence against them are hardly ever brought to justice. Some of this can be accounted for by poor treatment from police who often serve as the first responders to a crime. Sex worker NGO Zi Teng records that in Hong Kong, from January to April 2019 alone, there were nine cases where male police officers forced sex workers to service them, 268 cases of arbitrary arrest, as well as seven cases of indecent assault and threats.[6] Sex workers often choose not to make any report of the injustice they suffer because of stigmatization and because they fear not being believed or considered worthy of justice.

The aim of this book is to raise awareness of this unjust situation, and also to take my guild of biblical interpreters to task for how they have interpreted the word "prostitute" in the Bible in such a way that many readers continue to stigmatise sex workers and—perhaps unwittingly—to promote their victimization. Scholars and general readers of the Bible need to acknowledge that this sustains rape culture, and then find ways to identify and resist unjust and oppressive practices, including when they are targeted at sex workers. This is both a feminist and a human rights issue.

This study examines the Hong Kong context. Recently, Hong Kong gained international attention when over a million protesters took to the streets on 10 June 2019, protesting against the extradition bill and the ever-increasing presence and control of the Chinese government in the region. The protests continue, despite the threat of the epidemic of Coronavirus (COVID-19), arising in January 2020. Hong Kong was once a British colony, but in 1997 was recognised as a Special Administrative Region of China. It has been an important international economic centre and financial hub but its significant economic status has become compromised due to the ongoing protests. "West meets East" has often been used to describe Hong Kong and it is characterised as a place with a Western outlook but as Chinese at its core.

While I was still teaching at the Chinese University of Hong Kong, I embarked on a project of reading passages of the Hebrew Bible with female sex workers in the city. I focused on biblical passages where words from the Hebrew root *znh*, translated as "prostitute", occur.[7] In this book, I use the word "prostitute" to refer to those occurrences in the Bible, and "sex worker" to refer to those whose profession is selling sex. I started out on this project by volunteer-teaching English for JJJ in 2012–13. The project is inspired by Avaren Ipsen's, published in her monograph *Sex Working and the Bible*, where Ipsen reads stories about prostitutes from the Bible with female sex workers who are also activists in the San Francisco Bay area.[8] Her project uses the voices of contemporary sex workers to speak about and for the prostitutes in the Bible. Hence, where biblical authors and many interpreters might suppress prostitutes' voices, the sex workers of San Francisco make them heard. Because sex work is widely criminalised in the USA, where laws are often "informed by the Bible",[9] Ipsen's project embodies activism and aims to debunk the negative force of many biblical interpretations.

The Hong Kong context is different from that of California in a number of ways. In Hong Kong, sex work is not criminalised and is governed by laws that claim to regulate violence and maintain societal ethics. Moreover, the female sex workers I have come to know through JJJ do not identify themselves as activists, nor are they familiar with the Bible and the stories in it.[10] The outcome of my first reading of 1 Kings 3:16–28 ("The Judgment of Solomon") made me realise how biblical interpreters and commentators and even the biblical authors themselves missed the mark completely in their portrayal of sex workers. I am persuaded that this is because they do not know about sex work or the lives of sex workers, and I have raised this in an earlier publication.[11] In this book, through standpoint theory (explained below), I am evoking the voices of Hong Kong sex workers to reinterpret three Bible stories. My purpose is first, to highlight how ignorance has promoted discrimination and rape culture; second, to enhance understanding about sex work and sex workers' lives; and third, to actively challenge and rectify sex worker stigmatization and victimization.

1.2 Standpoint theory

Standpoint theory has its origins in feminist studies. It developed when philosophers and theorists acknowledged the success of feminist studies in pointing out that socio-political and economic power structures are involved in generating knowledge. As a consequence, knowledge is no longer regarded as objective and representative of reality.[12] On the contrary, perspectives from marginalised groups in a society generate more realistic, accurate and valuable information with regard to knowledge.

Sandra Harding in her book *The Feminist Standpoint Theory Reader*, elaborates as follows:

> Standpoint theories argue for "starting off thought" from the lives of marginalized peoples; beginning in those determinate, objective locations in any social order [that] will generate illuminating critical questions that do not arise in thought that begins from dominant group lives. Starting off research from women's lives will generate less partial and distorted accounts not only of women's lives but also of men's lives and of the whole social order. Women's lives and experiences provide the "grounds" for this knowledge, though these clearly do not provide foundations for knowledge in the conventional philosophical sense. These grounds are the site, the activities, from which scientific questions arise.[13]

Harding clarifies that standpoint theory does not disregard conventional and existent knowledge; instead, it adds to and supplements the production of knowledge. Standpoint theory challenges conventional claims of objectivity and authority highlighting that marginalised perspectives have not been allowed to critique and question the reason and consequences of their oppression and/or suppression. These latter perspectives, previously undervalued or ignored, warrant attention that can, nonetheless, be subjected to "scientific observation" and be validated.[14] K. McClure redefines the term "scientific" with reference to standpoint theory, so that it no longer signifies the allegedly "objective" body of knowledge determined by male-dominated institutions but instead a political consciousness that is reflective of an involved party's power relations to the subject of study.[15] Hence, standpoint theory is not merely about taking the perspectives of the marginalised and oppressed as the starting point of questioning things, but its goal is to question what causes their oppression and marginalization, and why these persist. Standpoint theory is therefore political. It exposes the dominant rationale as oppressive and compels it to recognise the value of the marginalised and of their perspectives as crucial to assembling complete knowledge. It also advocates for the full participation of the marginalised, as equally deserving of their share in humanity, and for fair and equal treatment and justice. Feminist standpoint theory has been successfully applied, developed and adapted to study the lives of women from different cultures, geographical locations, social strata and also from specific arenas within a community in a determined historical period.[16]

For the purpose of comparing the methodologies for studying the marginalised as subjects, I have considered, besides standpoint theory, postcolonialism and intersectionality. Amanda Gouws differentiates the epistemologies of standpoint theory and postcolonialism in that the latter tends to represent subaltern women as homogenous, failing to consider fully the diverse cultures from which women come.[17] In contrast, standpoint theory takes more seriously components such as race, ethnic and social status, as well as women's economic and cultural contexts, regardless of whether they are the subject or object of research. But standpoint theory has been criticised for its limitations in considering the multiple identities of an individual in a pluralistic society such as the theory of intersectionality does.[18] Standpoint theory, like postcolonialism, seems to be binary, concerned with the relationship of those *in* power vis-à-vis those who are *not*. Intersectionality, contrastingly, is more nuanced, in that it considers the oppressed in terms of the multiple levels of their power and oppression within a given society.

Standpoint theory is, however, better suited to my project than intersectionality, because I am not considering the multiple identities of sex workers per se, but rather the perspectives that arise from the profession of sex work. Standpoint theory enables me most effectively to study alongside sex workers the origin and consequences of their work, as well as the wide economic and social disparities this work creates. In doing so, it acknowledges diversity of experience alongside shared experiences. Ipsen's project, which has inspired mine, also employs standpoint theory. With the purpose of her project being to harness activism towards decriminalising sex work, standpoint theory compels Ipsen to question the origin both of sex work as portrayed in the biblical texts and of sex work in today's USA. In doing so, she engages the subjects of capitalism and corrupt economy, again both in the biblical texts and in the contemporary USA. Ipsen highlights the fact that sex work in both settings exists due to disparity of income and power. She goes on to take US politicians and the wealthy to task for the injustices that criminalization forces on sex workers. It is economic oppression, from which the wealthy and political class benefit, which must, she argues, bear much of the shame of crimes perpetrated against sex workers.

My work is also political and feminist but it departs from Ipsen's in that I will not dwell on the economic features of either the biblical or contemporary context. I do not deny the significance of economic conditions by any means,[19] but will focus instead on the deep-seated stigmatization shared by both prostitutes in the Bible and sex workers in the Hong Kong society of today, as well as on how related literatures (biblical interpretation and news media) promote rape culture—albeit possibly unwittingly. So, Ipsen takes politicians and economic influencers to task for criminalising sex workers by drawing parallels to biblical texts. In this book, I take to task the biblical authors, as well as the numerous interpreters of the Bible, of the past and present, from both Western and Chinese scholarship, because they have promoted rape culture, including in Hong Kong and in the context of Chinese Christianity. This has added to the victimization and vulnerability of modern-day sex workers. Through standpoint theory, the experiences and voices of Hong Kong sex workers will be heard. This work voices their perspectives, facilitated through their readings of biblical stories—and, in turn, those perspectives critique and illuminate how the biblical portrayal of prostitution and its interpretation are problematic.

1.3 The three biblical stories and the reading exercises

As already mentioned, this project is based on data collated from biblical readings I conducted with female Hong Kong sex workers. All are members of the JJJ Association. Each reading focused on a discrete text: 1 Kings 3:16–28 (on 5 August 2014) with five sex workers; Genesis 38 (on 15 February 2017) in two separate groups of six; and Hosea 1–3 (on 10 January 2018) with seven. Participants were informed and assured prior to the reading session that maintaining their confidentiality and anonymity was paramount. No one was called on at any point, let alone obliged to contribute, if they did not feel comfortable. Any participant was free to leave at any point. Immediately before the reading groups met, I repeated the conditions and assurances. I also promised participants that no names or identifiers would be mentioned in my records or publications: I would merely say, for example, "a few" or "most of the sex workers" or "three out of five felt this way", and so on. To maximise confidentiality and trust and to facilitate openness, I did not use a recording device but set down all responses in pen and ink. After each reading session, participants had full access to what I had written and all works published making any reference to them have been and will be made available in the JJJ Association office.

After conditions had been agreed, sex worker participants were encouraged to ask any questions they liked about the texts, the background of the texts and other related matters they felt were important to help them understand the text. Since the sex workers in the groups did not read the Bible or have much familiarity with it, I presented a brief background account to each text. For example, for 1 Kings 3:16–28, I explained who Solomon was and his significance in the Bible; for Genesis 38 I talked about the levirate custom and the importance of Judah as Israel's patriarch and as the ancestor in Jesus' lineage; and for Hosea 1–3 I spoke of the role of prophets and the features of literary prophetic writing, and I gave a brief historical background to Hosea 1–3.

In this book, I present these readings in the following order: the narrative of Tamar in Genesis 38; the story of the two prostitutes and King Solomon in 1 Kings 3:16–28 and the story of Gomer and the female prostitution figures in Hosea 1–3. In the course of this a number of things emerge. These include: what rape culture is and how its manifestations often bypass the radar of detection (e.g. when a revered person is the perpetrator of injustice); how power dynamics can transpire in a victim's plight being ignored; and how stigmatization and victimization of sex workers are justified in the Bible and elsewhere.

1.4 Synopsis

This introductory chapter has laid out the aims and the theoretical framework that inform this study. Pivotal to my endeavour is the confrontation of a specific feature of rape culture: namely, the victimization and stigmatization of certain individuals who are perceived as promiscuous and therefore as more dispensable and as deserving of punishment in the form of physical abuse, violence and rape. Deploying standpoint theory, I am mobilising the voices and the lived experiences of sex workers against this notion of rape culture. The sites of engagement of this mobilization are three biblical texts that mention sex work: Genesis 38; 1 Kings 3:16–28; and Hosea 1–3.

Chapter 2 paints the props for the stage. It provides a thumbnail portrait of the background to what rape culture is like in Hong Kong. It summarises laws and statistics and the extent of rape culture in local society and also in churches. This is followed by an account of the campaigners against rape culture. Next is the background of our characters: the Hong Kong sex workers. I will begin with introducing the NGOs for sex workers and detailing the support they provide. Then, I will present a general profile of sex workers and of the laws governing sex work in Hong Kong as well as how these impact sex work.

For Chapters 3 to 5, I present a brief description of the three biblical narratives, followed by a summary of the conventional interpretations found in readily available commentaries and works in Chinese penned by Hong Kong scholars and writers that are relied on by the local laity.[20] Using standpoint theory, I then discuss the readings with the sex workers and compare their insights to some interpretations from selected scholarship. Next, I summarise and highlight the points that contribute to the theme of this book: namely, how texts and interpretations promote rape culture. More specifically I examine, too, how rape myths have adversely influenced prejudice against Hong Kong sex workers.

In Chapter 3 I collate the sex workers' views that Genesis 38 is a rape text. They also observe how the story is silent about the reality of the rape culture that must have existed then. In addition, the sex workers' standpoints on the biblical usage of *qdsh* also reveal and unpack the likelihood of deeply held prejudices against their biblical counterparts in numerous interpretations. Most brilliantly of all, the sex workers fought against the attempts in the story to marginalise Tamar and themselves, and they argue v.14, where Tamar dons her disguise, is the crux of the story, not v.26, where Judah confesses Tamar is more righteous than he.

Chapter 4 is on the sex workers' reading of 1 Kings 3:16–28 and shows how the story evokes all the horrifying memories of their encounters with the police and the law courts, even if it is not overtly a rape text. The sex workers' standpoints show how this story is subversive, speaking against "them" and their children. They also notice how the story seems to support the police stigmatization and victimization of them and their ilk so that they often have to comply with rape and other bullying when facing threats of violence, even from men who owe them protection.

In Chapter 5, the sex workers' loathing of this rape text of Hosea 1–3 is reported. From the sex workers' standpoint, Christian interpretations can be seen to justify physical abuse, rape, victimization and marginalization of sex workers, thereby perpetuating rape culture against sex workers in the minds of Christian readers.

Chapter 6 summarises the significant points covered in the earlier chapters and draws conclusions looking forward to fulfilling my goal of challenging biblical scholars to reconsider how many of them interpret the Bible from rape culture supportive perspectives, whether they realise it or not. This often-hidden attitude must be revealed and eliminated because it can produce violence and hate crimes.

Notes

1 Jasmine Siu, "Hong Kong Rapist Who Researched Robbing Prostitutes Online Jailed for 11 Years", *South China Morning Post*, 11 October 2017. Retrieved from: https://www.scmp.com/news/hongkong/lawcrime/article/2115081/hong-kong-rapist-who-researched-robbing-prostitutes-online. The approximate currency exchange rate is rounded to the nearest US dollar, and the figures are taken as of 26 February 2020.

2 The following links lead to the comments mentioned here: https://bit.ly/2yMfoWz and http://hk.apple.nextmedia.com/realtime/news/20171012/57322192.
3 The transliteration for Cantonese 姐姐 is "jei jei", which refers to an elder sister and can denote either the singular or plural. The addition of 仔 "jai", which follows, refers to sex workers. Among themselves, the sex workers tend to call one another "sisters". My interview with Ms Sherry Hui, the coordinator for JJJ, on the subject of rape was conducted on 3 April 2019.
4 See note 1 above.
5 On legal definitions of rape and for rape in court settings, see Anniken Lucia Willumsen Laake and Cynthia Calkins, "Rape Culture", *The SAGE Encyclopedia of Psychology and Gender* (Kevin L. Nadal; London/New Delhi, Singapore: SAGE Publications, 2017), 1403–4.
6 For details, see *The 64th Issue of Zi Teng Newsletter*, 16 April 2019. The 65th issue, published on 24 August 2019, records a significantly lower incidence of crimes committed by police officers against sex workers, but a hike in crimes by clients, including 70 cases of theft and 30 cases of impersonating police. The decrease in police crimes and violence against sex workers can be attributed to the deployment of police officers to protest sites in Hong Kong during continuing pro-democracy demonstrations. Unfortunately, other sex-related crimes by police as part of these protests are duly reported. Raquel Carvalho, "Thousands Gather at #MeToo Rally to Demand Hong Kong Police Answer Accusations of Sexual Violence Against Protesters", *South China Morning Post*, 28 August 2019. Retrieved from: https://www.scmp.com/news/hong-kong/politics/article/3024789/thousands-gather-metoo-rally-demand-hong-kong-police-answer. Zi Teng is an NGO for sex workers. See Chapter Two, 2.4.2. In the 63rd issue, it was reported that crimes and violence against sex workers by police in the year 2018 amounted to 870 cases. For the above reports found in Zi Teng's newsletter, cf. http://www.ziteng.org.hk/eng/ newsletter.
7 The letters *znh* transliterate זנה, the biblical Hebrew root word for meanings related to "prostitution", both literally and figuratively. Words of this root occur in the Hebrew Bible 139 times. Most of the occurrences appear in prophetic literature to depict the unfaithful behaviour of countries, especially Israel. In this way idolatry and allegiance to gods other than YHWH is depicted, metaphorically, as "prostitution", as well as adultery. There are only a few references where the word designates female characters: Tamar (Genesis 38:15); Rahab (Joshua 2:1; 6:17, 22–23, 25); Jephthah's mother (Judges 11:1); Samson's friend (Judges 16:1); the two unnamed women in Solomon's court (1 Kings 3:18). For the reference to Gomer as a prostitute, see Chapter Five. Cf. S. Erlandsson, "זנה", *Theological Dictionary of the Old Testament* vol. IV, 99–104; and David J.A. Clines (ed.), "זנה I", and "זנונים", *Dictionary of Classical Hebrew* vol. III (Sheffield: Sheffield Academic, 1996), 121–3 and 123 respectively.
8 Avaren Ipsen, *Sex Working and the Bible* (London: Equinox, 2009).
9 Ipsen, cf. 1–5; 32–3.
10 There is no study on the specific religious backgrounds of Hong Kong sex workers. However, Buddhism and Taoism are the two most popular religions in Hong Kong (cf. Home Affairs Bureau, "Hong Kong: The Facts; Religion and Customs". Published May 2016. Retrieved from: https://www.gov.hk/en/about/abouthk/factsheets/docs/religion.pdf.) This was borne out, too, by the religious affiliation of the sex workers with whom I conducted this project. The majority of the sex

workers who came from Mainland China, when asked about affiliation, said they do not have a religion. It was evident when reading stories from the Bible that these were new to the sex workers.

11 Nancy Tan, "Hong Kong Sex Workers: Mothers Reading 1 Kgs 3:16–28", in *Honoring the Past, Looking to the Future: Essays from the 2014 International Congress of the Ethnic Chinese Biblical Scholars*, eds. Gale Yee and Y.H. Yieh (Hong Kong: Divinity School of Chung Chi College, The Chinese University of Hong Kong, 2016), 157–75.

12 Sandra Harding, "Introduction: Standpoint Theory as a Site of Political, Philosophic, and Scientific Debate", in *The Feminist Standpoint Theory Reader: Intellectual and Political Controversies*, ed. Harding (NY/London: Routledge, 2004), 1–15.

13 Harding, "Rethinking Standpoint Epistemology: What is 'Strong Objectivity?'" in *The Feminist Standpoint Reader*, 128.

14 Ibid., 132–7.

15 K. McClure, "The Issue of Foundations: Scientised Politics, Politicised Science, and Feminist Critical Practice", in *Feminists Theorise the Political*, eds. J. Butler and J. W. Scott (New York: Routledge, 1992), 34.

16 For a discussion and examples, see Yin Paradies, "Whither Standpoint Theory in a Post-Truth World?". *Cosmopolitan Civil Societies* 10.2 (2018): 119–29. Retrieved from: http://dx.doi.org/10.5130/ccs.v10i2.5980. Paradies cites the following recent works using standpoint theory: T. Fattore, J. Mason, and E. Watson, *Children's Understandings of Well-Being: Towards a Child Standpoint* (Dordrecht: Springer, 2016); J. Gilroy and M. Donelly, "Australian Indigenous People with Disability: Ethics and Standpoint Theory", in *Disability in the Global South: The Critical Handbook*, eds. S. Grech and K. Soldatic (Cham: Springer, 2016), 545–66. https://doi.org/10.1007/978-3-319- 42488-0_35; and A. Moreton-Robinson, "Towards an Australian Indigenous Women's Standpoint Theory: A Methodological Tool", *Australian Feminist Studies* 28.78 (2013): 331–47. Retrieved from: doi: 10.1080/08164649.2013.876664.

17 Amanda Gouws, "Feminist Epistemology and Representation: The Impact of Postmodernism and Postcolonialism", *Transformation* 30 (1996): 65–82.

18 Paradies, 120–5.

19 On economic considerations and sex work in Hong Kong, see "Compensated Dating in Hong Kong", *Time Out Hong Kong*, 24 May 2016. Retrieved from: https://www.timeout.com/hong-kong/blog/compensated-dating-in-hong-kong-052416.

20 The Protestant churches in Hong Kong are mostly evangelical. There is a limited selection of publishers that churches would recommend for the congregation. Those that I have selected do not include the translated works by Western scholars and writers (who are themselves evangelicals). Academic works are rarely promoted in churches or carried by the popular bookstores in Hong Kong—since most of the owners of these bookstores are evangelical Christians themselves.

2 Rape culture and sex work in Hong Kong

Over a decade ago, in the years 2008–9, Hong Kong was stunned and sex workers gripped with fear when a series of murdered sex workers were discovered in their one-roomed flat brothels.[1] According to the statistics reported in 2009, 36 murders were committed in Hong Kong in 2008, of which six victims were female sex workers. When interviewed by *Time*, Elaine Tam, the then director of Zi Teng (an NGO for sex workers), explained how sex workers are widely stigmatised and viewed as "bad" people in society, and that consequently, killing them seemed almost to be justified.[2] The irrational belief that sex workers are immoral and, therefore, deserving of punishment, including physical abuse, rape and extortion, unfortunately persists.

This chapter will give a brief and general background to illuminate some of the context-specific topics covered in this book. These include: how the judicial system in Hong Kong defines rape, a comparison of police reports on rape incidents with the reports from NGOs for victims of sexual crimes, and a brief report on the contribution of SlutWalk Hong Kong, which raised awareness of what rape culture is. I will also provide some other information on matters related to sex work in Hong Kong: the recent reports of crimes against sex workers, information on NGOs for sex workers, and a general profile of what sex work is like in Hong Kong. These accounts will flesh out what the social, political and judicial environment in which Hong Kong sex workers ply their trade is like.

2.1 Rape laws in Hong Kong

The laws defining rape are categorised under a broader section called "Sexual Offences" and in the sub-section "Non-consensual Sexual Offences"; the Crimes Ordinance (Cap 200) and under Section 118(3). There, rape is defined in gender-specific terms as penile penetration of a vagina; hence, males are envisaged as perpetrators and only females are imagined as victims of rape.[3] There is no acknowledgement of male rape. The following conditions must be proven for a crime to qualify as rape:

a   he has unlawful sexual intercourse with a woman who at the time of the intercourse does not consent to it; and
b   at that time he knows that she does not consent to the intercourse or he is reckless as to whether she consents to it.[4]

The law also makes clear that all the above must be proven beyond doubt in court: i.e. that no consent was granted on the woman's part, unless, perhaps, she was under duress to grant consent.[5] As long as other circumstances can prove that a man accused of rape was led to believe that consent had been granted, he cannot be convicted. A further provision was made that, under certain circumstances, should a woman be deceived into engaging in sexual intercourse, then evidence must be presented to prove the deception. This offence, however, falls under another part of the law in Section 121 where the victim is described as being "drugged to perform unlawful sexual acts"—though not necessarily rape.[6] These qualifications and refinements seem to have been made because the maximum conviction for rape is currently lifetime imprisonment. In effect, the law has introduced gradations, or "less" and "more" serious cases of rape.

The section "Non-consensual sexual offences" also includes other sexual offences such as "indecent assault", "buggery" and "procuring an unlawful sexual act by threats or intimidation". Each category specifies the extent of the act. All other non-consensual sexual acts that do not involve penile penetration of the vagina fall under "indecent assault". The maximum conviction for indecent assault is ten years. The element of "consent" is the basic criterion for this category.

There are likely to be emendations to the above categories and their penalties in the near future, as the Law Reform Commission of Hong Kong announced on 5 December 2019 that recommendations have been made to amend rape law.[7] Basically, the term "rape" will be dropped and replaced with "sexual offence without consent". This will include all penile penetration of the vagina, as well as the mouth or anus. As for other forms of penetration, such as with objects, these are to be classified under a new category called "gender-neutral sexual offences". It will also change the term from "indecent assault" to "sexual assault". New laws have also been created to protect minors and persons with mental impairment from offences like "sexual grooming" because with both a person's ability to give consent can be compromised. Sexual offences such as incest, exposure and bestiality, among others, have also been refined and adapted.

It seems that the laws are no longer so fixated on heteronormative discourses that view sex solely in terms of penile penetration, and of the vagina only. Instead, definitions of what constitutes sex are becoming broader and more gender inclusive. This reflects more societal acknowledgement that sexual crimes can be perpetrated by and against both males and females. There is also more of a sense that sexual minorities are no longer being ignored or passed over quite so lightly. These changes are definitely improvements on the earlier wording of the laws and the final formulation with penalties may be looked forward to with some optimism. RainLily, an NGO providing shelter and support for victims of rape and sexual assault, welcomes the changes but is also disappointed to have to point out neglect in categorising "image-based sexual abuse" as a crime—that is, offences related to circulating personal images with sexual content without consent (e.g. revenge porn).[8]

2.2 Rape statistics in Hong Kong

According to the statistics most recently released by the Hong Kong Police Force, there were 50 cases of rape in 2019, 63 in 2018, 65 in 2017, 71 in 2016, 70 in 2015 and 56 in 2014.[9] The statistics show a steady decrease in number over the years 2014–19, with a peak in 2016. However, these figures only account for the number of reported rapes and do not account for other matters, such as the number of cases where investigations were aborted, cases prosecuted, etc. To exemplify the real issue, the following report which was released in 2018 by the Hong Kong Police Force will suffice.

On 17 January 2018, at the Legislative Council Meeting, a question was raised concerning why there was an increase in the cases of rape and sexual assault when comparing the same periods of Jan–Oct 2016 and 2017, following questions related to the administration of handling such cases. Apparently, there was an increase of 9.8% for rape and 9.2% for indecent assault.[10] (The report did not supply the exact number of rape cases for Jan–Oct 2016.) The reply, assuring that protocols have been made to provide better administration for handling such offences, was made with some supporting statistics from the Hong Kong Police.

For purposes of clarity, the statistics pertaining only to rape will be captured for study here. Table 2.1 accounts for the number of persons arrested, prosecuted and convicted in a given year through the period 2013 to September 2017. Therefore, it must be noted that the figures in 2017 should be taken with caution when used for comparison because

Table 2.1: Statistics on rape for the period 2013–17 (January to September)[11]

	2013	2014	2015	2016	2017 (January to September)
Rape (Section 118 of the Crimes Ordinance)					
Number of persons arrested	106	62	70	65	43
Number of persons prosecuted	62	43	33	29	19
Number of persons convicted	18	17	10	6	10

they do not account for the whole year. At the same time, each category does not directly correlate to the cases accounted for, due to the duration of time required for investigation and arrest, and for prosecution. In other words, for example, the 29 persons prosecuted in 2016 are not necessarily among the 65 arrested in 2016.

From Table 2.1, we observe that there is a decline in the number of persons arrested over a period of nearly five years, just after the year 2014. This decline seems to correlate to the number of persons prosecuted. The figures show that in the period of four complete years between 2013–16, 2014 seems to stand out. Comparatively speaking, it records the least number of arrests and a high number of persons convicted for rape. After 2014, the figures on the numbers of persons convicted drop drastically. And, in 2016, we see that only six persons were convicted. While we may not take the figure in 2017 as accurate, we do find a decrease in the number of persons prosecuted, and a higher number of persons convicted compared to 2016. Nonetheless, these figures also show that the number of convictions is much lower than the number of persons arrested and prosecuted, even if we take into account more liberally that a case might take three to five years from prosecution to conviction.

These statistics and reports only provide a glimpse of Hong Kong police and judicial responses to the cases of reported rapes. It is common knowledge that many cases of rape and sexual assault go unreported, especially when the victims are sex workers. More of the issue will be uncovered below.

2.3 Rape culture and resistance in Hong Kong

The figures and reports in Table 2.1 only give us a glimpse into the bigger picture, which is, unfortunately, similar to the situation in many cities. The large discrepancy between the number of persons arrested and finally convicted is a good indication that many of the rape cases prosecuted result in acquittal without charge and that most rapists go free.[12]

The determining factor in the rape laws is proof of non-consent. Non-consent must be proven beyond doubt and often the victim's personal life comes under scrutiny, looking at everything from how she (in most cases) relates to her friends, peers and persons of the opposite sex, to her dress and sexual history. These matters can be brought out in open court with a view to casting doubt on a victim's claims of non-consent and to imply that she must or may have hinted that she *did* give consent or, at least, that she did not explicitly refuse sex. Online news media also report on victims' personal backgrounds, sometimes giving details about mode of dressing, the kind of friends she has, former partners, etc. regardless of whether the verdict has been reached.[13] Apparently, it is not difficult to find advertisements for law firms that assure potential clients who are being accused of rape that these attorneys can help defend the accused by creating doubt regarding non-consent. Thus, forces to be marshalled against a victim via victim-blaming and other rape myths are very much available to those accused of rape, albeit sometimes at a cost. These forces stand in opposition to laws that attempt to protect victims. This is the reality in Hong Kong and it is a highly visible indicator of rape culture. As the statistics indicate, rape is common (in all likelihood much more so than reported incidents suggest) but prosecutions do not result in convictions.

Catherine A. MacKinnon argues that "the law sees and treats women the way men see women".[14] The situation is not just the fact that "men rule women", but this "rule" functions and enacts in a "male way".[15] So, while the law recognises the grievousness of rape and accords a maximum penalty of life imprisonment, the conviction rate falls well below even the prosecution rate. Alongside this, there is evidence that victims' claims of "non-consent" are played down or overshadowed with doubt via the "male way". The procedures permit an emphasis on the male-oriented perception and interpretation of what constitutes "consent". Hence, the *perceived* outcomes of cases of rape that end in non-conviction are ultimately that the accused is not guilty, while the complainant has, by implication, "misled" the court, or lied. The male is acquitted of rape charges and the woman is stigmatised. She was the one who reported it and called it rape. During the prosecution not only is her personal sexual history exposed to scrutiny and judgement in court and in public, but she is also, at least implicitly, called a liar. When a victim of rape goes to court and the rapist is not convicted, on the grounds of insufficient proof, then the law has not only failed to protect the victim but has publicly cast her as the instigator of a rape allegation. She is blamed for not making her "non-consent" *apparent beyond doubt* and for not being able to prove absence of consent.

The fact that so many rapists go free after arrest and prosecution is one of the main reasons why many more cases of rape go unreported. RainLily, the NGO that provides crisis services ranging from medical and psychological to legal, as well as support related to the consequences of sexual assault and rape, estimates that "one in seven women in HK is a victim of sexual violence".[16] The figure here refers to all women aged 14 years old and above.[17] It has also been observed and acknowledged that the dominant voices in Hong Kong education and public media prefer to avoid the subject of sex.[18] The effect of this is a climate where the language to talk about sex and sexual violation is deficient and this becomes another obstacle to victims reporting.[19] In addition, victims struggle to report an assailant especially when the latter might hold a high status in society, which might result in doubting a victim's claims and, worse, might draw even more public attention and judgement on a victim. When rape or sexual assault victims attempt to report, one of the common responses is questioning a victim to find out whether they realise the impact that such an accusation will have on the well-being of the accused and his family.

RainLily has raised further concerns that implicate the police and judicial system in the prevalence of a "victim-blaming culture" that has transpired in the low figures of rape conviction in 2017.[20] Victims also report feeling their integrity being stripped from them and a sense of immense shame towards/about their violated bodies. Also very damaging is the traditional Chinese belief that victims of rape and sexual violence bring defamation and contempt to their family's honour. This erstwhile common view is often portrayed in Chinese films and drama, and reflects the Qing period (1644–1912) during which suicide was recommended for the victim of rape for the sake of her family and memory.[21] Sadly, the ethos of those days stipulated that a victim should not cease in resisting the ordeal of rape at every point, even if she should risk injury and death. That draconian attitude to rape effectively passed the death penalty on victims at the point of being attacked. This grave example of a rape culture firmly rejected survivors.

The Christian Church community can be another locus where rape myths are propagated. For example, in local churches, female members from their adolescent years on are taught to dress "decently" and "modestly"—to avoid apparel that is figure-hugging and/or exposes or may expose more skin, such as short dresses or skirts, mini-skirts and hot-pants, and/or low necklines and/or back. This is because they should not cause the male members of their church "to stumble" thereby leading them into temptation and to sin against God (sometimes citing Romans 14:21). A survey on sexual harassment conducted by the Hong Kong

Christian Council[22] in the Protestant churches, during the period from August 2017 to April 2018, states that 55 cases were reported: 55 cases in which 35 of the perpetrators were church pastors or leaders.[23] To collect the data, participating churches disseminated the survey to church members and forms were returned in the church or to the investigator directly. At a live conference held on 24 June 2018, Jessica Tso, the lead investigator, reported that most of the churches refused to participate. The most widely cited reasons were: 1) no case had ever been reported; 2) the church would never have any case of sexual harassment; and 3) such surveys would create disharmony and unrest among members. One of the church leaders stated during the conference that Tso was "making a mountain out of a molehill since out of about 1300 protestant churches … [only] 55 cases were reported". He claimed that the figure was "insignificant". Some attendees concurred. This was considered by other attendees and Tso to be one of the most regrettable comments made at the conference. The published report also highlights how most cases were swept under the carpet when they came to the attention of leadership personnel. Many of the Church Board accused victims of trying to bring harm to those accused, especially when they held leadership positions.[24] This explains why most cases go unreported, as with cases of rape in society at large. The churches in general tend to safeguard their mostly male leaders in the hierarchy within the institution, to the detriment of the rights of the victims of rape and sexual offences, even when they, too, are church members or adherents. The process of this research and the response from some of Hong Kong's church leaders show that the Christian Church is another culprit in perpetuating rape myths, promoting rape culture and even breeding and protecting culprits. At the end of the report, the Christian Council committee recommended that Hong Kong churches need an independent investigation into the 55 cases reported. Perhaps with this proposed investigation many more who have been silenced, thinking they are trying to be "better Christians" according to their leaders' persuasion, will come forward with their stories.[25]

Thankfully, there are NGOs like RainLily that have acted as advocates for victims of sexual crimes and have helped in resisting rape culture. Another campaign called "SlutWalk" has also contributed to raising awareness of the issue. SlutWalk began in Toronto, Canada in 2011 when, during a routine visit to Osgoode Hall Law School to advise students on personal safety, Michael Sanguinetti, a police constable, warned women against "dressing like sluts" to avoid rape. This provoked some students to protest against victim-blaming.[26] The protest inspired many more in Canada and the USA to join and, as it grew, it became an international movement. Angie Ng, a victim of sexual violence turned feminist activist, started SlutWalk in Hong Kong later in the same year.[27] Since then, Ng has organised the event annually in Hong Kong. Ng has commented in an interview that the protest's participants in Hong Kong had, to begin with, been mostly limited to university students, but that others were beginning to join the march.[28] She is seeing signs that the wider public is now becoming more aware of what rape culture and victim-blaming are, due in large part to the upsurge of personal experiences of sexual harassment and abuse disclosed and made public through the digital activist #MeToo movement.[29] Over the years, publicity has made clear to the public that participants of SlutWalk are supporters of victims of rape and sexual violence, activists against victim-blaming and debunkers of rape myths. Participants are not, of course, necessarily victims themselves—nor are they women deserving of criticism on account of their sexual desires or consenting practices. Instead of "sluts" labelling women who are denigrated on account of prejudices against them, the word has, in the SlutWalk, been reclaimed to make clear that women can make their own choices in terms of what they do and wear and that none of these choices invite or justify sexual violence.

These are all positive signs of progress but more conscious efforts are still needed to re-educate those who adhere to entrenched misogynistic attitudes and beliefs, as well as to gender stereotyping and the propagation of rape myths. The increasing pressure in Hong Kong of Chinese authoritarian rule, which endorses more traditional Chinese "values" that promote binary constructions of gender and insist on a heteronormative outlook for society, is extremely worrying.[30] China revised its censorship laws for all television programmes in 2016, restricting how female actors may dress and behave. There is to be no portrayal of "homosexuality", and no negative portrayal of those in authority. The reason given for this is to safeguard the political infrastructures of the country.[31] This stance demonstrates China's tight reign and authoritarian or paternalistic control over how gender and sexuality may be expressed. This stance also comes at the additional cost of further promoting rape myths, in particular, the myth that people in authority do not commit sexual crimes and that only women get raped because of what they wear and how they behave. Interestingly, this is the same ethos shared with numerous leaders of local churches, as discussed above. All these cultural moves seem to be aimed at undoing efforts towards a more conscientiously socially accepting and inclusive society.

What we have observed so far is that, even with rape laws in place, victims' bodies and experiences are denied justice because the enactment of laws does not seriously take into account the standpoint of those who are suffering, and actually excuses acts of violence against them through maneuvered legal procedure. The society on the whole, from its culture to its laws and especially in local churches and other hierarchical locales, promotes rape culture rather than protests against it. Many adults remain ignorant on the subject and/or refuse to consider the consequences that victim-blaming brings down on victims of rape and sexual assault, regardless of gender. For all that it is worth, the recent outcry against police sexual violence towards female protesters in the ongoing Hong Kong democracy protests against China's efforts to control the region has raised public awareness of these issues.[32] That is, the public has suddenly been made aware of the violence of sexual harassment, as well as of the injustice of not acknowledging and addressing rape and other sexual offences when these are committed by people in authority. Perhaps widespread support and sympathy for the pro-democracy protests have finally also extended to those of its protesters who have endured sexual assault. Hopefully, this spread in awareness will also be translated into improving everyday lives beyond the framework of police violence.

2.4 Sex work in Hong Kong

In this section I will provide an outline of the laws regulating sex work in Hong Kong, followed by an explanation of the consequences of such laws and what they mean for sex workers. I will also introduce the NGOs supporting sex workers. But first, I will present a general profile of the composition of the population of Hong Kong sex workers.

2.4.1 General background information about sex workers

No one knows exactly how many sex workers there are in Hong Kong. None of the NGOs has to date successfully collated an accurate and comprehensive record. Zi Teng cites a source that estimates there to have been about 20,000–100,000 sex workers in 2001.[33] But there are some disagreements with this (imprecise) number. More conservative figures, based on the census for HIV prevention, put the figure at 10,000.[34] Recent research claims the numbers of sex workers have certainly escalated.[35] In 2017, Action for REACH OUT (AFRO) reported that in recent years there has been a demand for and surge of foreign sex workers who have come from "the Philippines, countries in Africa and South America, Brazil, Russia, and Eastern Europe".[36] Also, many Mainland Chinese sex workers regularly enter and leave Hong Kong. Their movement in and out of the region is unpredictable and while some work independently, others work for triad-linked syndicates.[37] There is also an increasingly prominent group of young sex workers who do not call themselves sex workers but simply describe themselves as "friends" participating in online "compensated dating".[38] Not to deny the presence of these groups, and recognising that these communities represent an important sector in the sex trade of Hong Kong, the study to follow will concentrate on sex workers with full residential rights in Hong Kong.

According to NGOs, the general profile of sex workers in Hong Kong comprises mainly women from Mainland China. JJJ estimates that about 75–8% of them attain rights of residence via marriage to locals.[39] The remaining 22–5% are native to Hong Kong. As for age distribution: 80% are between 31–50 years old; 12% 20–30 years old and 8% 50–60+ years old. In terms of educational qualifications, 35% of them completed their primary school education and another 35% completed their lower secondary school education; another 25% completed their higher secondary school education; and the remaining 5% attained a higher level of education. Of the 70% that form the lower education band—many of whom are from Mainland China—the majority are trained in specialised skills such as iron working. In Hong Kong, however, females do not work in these trades. Consequently, many of the migrants are not able to find a job for which they were trained and cannot afford to pay the fees to learn another skill or trade. With regard to marital status, only 5% are single, 40% are married and 55% are divorced. In addition, 90% of them are mothers. Sex working mothers are common throughout the rest of the world, but it seems that Hong Kong has a particularly high percentage. Ipsen pointed out regarding the sex workers of the Bay Area that almost all only became sex workers *after* motherhood.[40] The same applies to the Hong Kong setting as well.

2.4.2 Advocacy for sex workers in Hong Kong

Currently, there are five NGOs in Hong Kong protecting the rights of sex workers, namely: Midnight Blue, Teen's Key, Action for REACH OUT (AFRO), Zi Teng and Jei Jei Jai Association (JJJ). None of them are affiliated with any of the religious groups of Hong Kong, Christian or otherwise.

Midnight Blue began as a project extension from Zi Teng to cater to the needs of male and transgender sex workers, both in Hong Kong and Shenzhen, Mainland China. In 2006, it became established as an independent NGO.[41] Teen's Key is another off-shoot from Zi Teng that became an independent NGO in 2011. Teen's Key conducts outreach in the sex industry targeting the specific age group of young women aged 15–25 years old. The needs of this younger demographic are significantly different from those of their older counterparts—hence, the establishment of a separate NGO. Apparently, all the board members of Teen's Key are not older than 30 years old.[42]

The full name of AFRO is Action for Rights of Entertainers in Asia to Combat Human Oppression and Unjust Treatment. It was founded as an NGO in 1993 by Sister Ann Gray and Sister Helene O'Sullivan, Catholic nuns from the Missionary Sisters of Saint Columban, and an American woman named Melanie Orchant.[43] The three women started their outreach to sex workers in Mongkok in 1991, initially solely concerned with educating sex workers on health issues. In 1993, they opened their first drop-in centre at Yau Ma Tei. In 2007, AFRO became independent from the Mission. Its purpose is to advocate for equal rights of sex workers to legal services and to services safeguarding these rights, so that sex workers may "stand up and speak out for themselves".[44]

Zi Teng was founded in 1996 as the first centre for sex workers set up and run by persons from Hong Kong. The main founder, Ms Yim Yue Lin, and a group of volunteers from different backgrounds, including some social workers and church workers, contribute in different capacities to operate the centre.[45] Zi Teng shares the goals of AFRO, and offers services informing sex workers on both health and legal matters. Zi Teng is particularly active in the area of publication through all forms of media, churning out important and up-to-date information aimed at sex workers in both Chinese and English. It also publishes information educating the public about sex work and promoting the equal rights of sex workers. Zi Teng supports and makes accessible research and projects about sex work in both Hong Kong and other parts of the world.[46] It is the vision of both AFRO and Zi Teng that sex workers will themselves run the two NGOs one day.

JJJ is the first sex worker NGO that was set up and run by and for sex workers. JJJ began as a group initiated by Zi Teng in 2008, following the series of brutal murders of sex workers mentioned at the outset of this chapter. In 2010, JJJ became an NGO with its own centre independent from Zi Teng. The sex workers of JJJ engaged Ms Sherry Lai Kwan Hui to co-ordinate the operation. Alongside her leadership, JJJ also accepts volunteers and student interns to help run the centre. JJJ organises and co-ordinates programmes and publishes and disseminates bi-monthly newsletters, delivering these to sex workers' doorsteps. The content of these newsletters includes the most current news affecting sex work, including updates about suspicious and abusive clients at large, and announcements of the various courses and/or workshops offered and social gatherings organised by the abovementioned NGOs. Sometimes the newsletters also contain warnings about certain police officers at particular neighbourhoods. They also warn and remind sex workers about regular blood tests and check-ups for prevention or treatment of sexually transmitted diseases. The printed newsletters are important outreach tools especially for some sex workers who prefer privacy and also those new to the industry so that they know whom to contact should they need help in any way.

All the NGOs mentioned above provide similar and primary support on issues covering sexual health, protection, self-advancement and empowerment in terms of utilising legal knowledge and services. They regularly conduct workshops and seminars on these subjects. These NGOs, in protecting and supporting sex workers' rights and general well-being, are also the primary contact should a sex worker find herself hurt or in police custody. Because the laws in Hong Kong compel sex workers to conduct their services in solitary premises (as opposed to communal brothels), the NGOs also provide an important service in terms of forming sex worker community and solidarity. Through them, sex workers receive access to information, support and some peace of mind. The NGOs co-operate with each other and often work together for the benefit of sex workers. In particular, they keep each other up-to-date, especially when there is a crime reported by a sex worker.

2.4.3 Hong Kong laws governing sex work[47]

The Crime Ordinance Sections 130–14 stipulate the laws regulating sex work. Some of these are summarised below:

1. Anyone who holds an individual and "controls" their decisions for the purpose to, or engage them in sex work, regardless of locations—locally or abroad—will be incriminated (Crimes Ordinance Sections 130–1).
2. Anyone who lives off whether in part or fully the wages of sex workers will be prosecuted (Crimes Ordinance Section 137).
3. Anyone keeping a vice establishment—whether as a landlord or tenant by knowingly allowing their premises to be used for sex work can be convicted under this law (Crime Ordinance Sections 139–44).
4. Anyone found soliciting for sex in the public will be apprehended. In addition, advertising in public areas is also illegal (Crime Ordinance Section 147A–F).

Under the same section as the last cited law, it is also mentioned that male homosexual intercourse is considered "immoral" and subject to the same law for buggery.

2.4.4 Consequences of the laws regulating sex work

Although there is no law criminalising sex work, the laws in general prohibit the sites where sex work can take place. Thus, sex work is prohibited in hotels, brothels, nightclubs and massage parlours, as also is soliciting in public. This compels sex workers to conduct their trade solely in private flats, commonly called "one room one phoenix" establishments. The case of rape mentioned at the beginning of Chapter 1 and the murder cases referred to above indicate that, as a result, sex workers are more vulnerable to abuse and violence. In order to ensure some safety, it is common to find a cluster of "one room one phoenix" apartments in close proximity, either in a single building or in the same street. The most well-known place where the whole building has been renovated into one-room flats and rented out to sex workers is Fuij Building at Causeway Bay.[48] Unfortunately, these premises cannot remain permanent locations for sex workers, because landlords fear they may be indicted for criminal activities. Consequently, sex workers often have to relocate after a short period of time.

For the sake of security, every sex worker's "one room one phoenix" apartment has CCTV installed outside the entrance door. It also serves a secondary purpose as the sex worker behind the door can decide whether or not to accept a client. Sometimes there will be a few pictures of the sex workers placed outside the doors to the flats to tempt customers. Since advertising for sex work is strictly regulated by law, some landlords prohibit these displays.

In addition to the abovementioned laws, police have been given orders and leeway, with permission for "body contact", in order to "entrap" sex workers and to arrest them for soliciting.[49] The Hong Kong Police Force defends its actions with the claim that it is attempting to curb vice and to protect people who are trafficked or forced into the sex trade. It shows no sign of making an effort to discriminate between professional and criminal sex work. Human rights group Amnesty International has identified abuses resulting from police activities and has called for Hong Kong's laws to decriminalise sex work and better protect sex worker rights.[50]

The law forcing sex workers to rent private spaces imposes another hardship. Renting a room/flat in Hong Kong is a very daunting matter, because land is the priciest commodity there. The average rent for a 70-square-feet en suite flat in the city is in the range of HK$8,000–18,000 (US$1,030–2,330) a month.[51] The high cost of rent alone makes it clear that it is difficult for sex workers to make a living. Added to rent is also the high cost of living in the city, as well as high costs for childcare and health-related services. Furthermore, sex work is intensely competitive. Taking these financial and security factors into consideration, it is no wonder the NGOs deem the laws unfair to sex workers and they continue to lobby against them.

For all these challenges, sex work is still considered a lucrative job, comparatively speaking. It is the only trade that pays well and quickly where no educational qualification is required. Working hours are flexible and allow sex worker mothers to be parents to their children. Moreover, in this branch of the profession, there is no "boss" to answer to.

2.4.5 Section summary

The perils that come with sex work are many. In Hong Kong, these are exacerbated by the laws regulating sex work, which contribute to the likelihood of endangerment.[52] To summarise: sex workers are extremely vulnerable to physical abuse and violence, including rape and murder. In recent years, sex workers have also fallen victim to media-related crimes, where clients have taken pictures of sex workers and used these without their permission. Sex workers are often victims of theft and armed robbery and are prone to bullying by police, which is pervasive.[53] Police often treat sex workers with impunity and seem to consider it their duty to discipline and punish them. Hence, not only the general public but also law and order officials (both the police and legal professionals) make sex workers a target of victimization and stigmatization. What this chapter has covered is that the laws governing sexual crimes and rape have not been fair to victims. Not only are sex workers disproportionately prone to suffering sexual and other forms of physical violence, the laws governing their work also serve to make them vulnerable, including economically and physically. Rape culture is pervasive, including in Hong Kong. It has a profoundly negative impact on women but on sex workers in particular.

Whereas there are signs of more sympathy towards victims of sexual violence, as is evidenced by responses to #MeToo and growing participation in Hong Kong's SlutWalk, this has not extended to the multiple injustices suffered by sex workers. This book hopes to redress some of this injustice in a new way: through Bible stories about prostitution and through listening to the sex workers who have shared their standpoints on rape culture. Perhaps hearing these perspectives will make the plight and the valuable insights of sex workers more vivid. In turn, this will, I hope, lead to positive advocacy and action for sex workers, both in Hong Kong and beyond. Next, I will report on the first biblical story.

Notes

1 Deena Guzder, "Hong Kong Alarmed Over Sex-Workers Murders", *Time*, 10 February 2019. Retrieved from: http://content.time.com/time/world/article/0, 8599, 1878395,00.html.
2 Ibid.
3 "Sexual Offences", Community Legal Information Centre. (Law and Technology Centre, The University of Hong Kong). Retrieved from: http://www.clic.org.hk/en/topics/sexual offences/I_Non-consensual_Sexual_Offences/B_Rape/1_Elements_ of_the_offence/. This link provides ready access and is a more convenient reference in comparison with its source, which can be found at: http://www.hklii.hk/eng/hk/legis/ord/200/ under Part 12, Section 118.
4 Ibid.
5 Ibid.
6 "Non-consensual Sexual Offences", Community Legal Information Centre. (Law and Technology Centre, The University of Hong Kong). Retrieved from: http://www.clic.org.hk/en/topics/sexual_offences/I_Non-consensual_Sexual_ Offen ces/B_Rape/1_Elements_of_the_offence/b_Consent/i_Absence_of_consent/index.shtml.
7 "LRC Issues Report on Review of Substantive Sexual Offences", The Government of Hong Kong Special Administrative Region, *Press Releases*, 5 December 2019. Retrieved from: https://www.info.gov.hk/gia/general/201912/05/P2019120500374.htm.
8 RainLily (see also note 16, below) points out scope for further improvements. Cf. "Association Concerning Sexual Violence Against Women's Response on the Law Reform Commission's Release of Review of Substantive Sexual Offences", *RainLily*, 5 December 2019. Retrieved from: https://rainlily.org.hk/eng/news/2019/12/05/lrcreport.
9 "Crime Figures in Detail", Hong Kong Police Force (revised in March 2020). Retrieved from: https://www.police.gov.hk/ppp_en/09_statistics/csd.html.
10 "LCQ 20: Police Committed to Combating Sexual Offences", The Government of Hong Kong Special Administrative Region, *Press Releases*, 17 January 2018. Retrieved from: https://www.info.gov.hk/gia/general/201801/17 /P2018011700658.htm.
11 Ibid.
12 Rachel Blundy, "Hong Kong Police and Judicial System Accused of 'Victim Blaming Culture' as Rape Conviction Rate Falls: Campaigners Claim as Many as Nine in Ten Do Not Report Their Attackers", *South China Morning Post*, 18 February 2017. Retrieved from: https://www.scmp.com/news/hong-kong/article/2071838/hong-kong-police-and-judicial-system-accused-victim-blaming-culture.
13 Catherine Lai, "In Pictures: 'Enough of Rape Myths'—Hong Kong Protestors March Against Sexual Violence", *Hong Kong Free Press*, 21 November 2017. Retrieved from: https://www.hongkongfp.com/2017/11/21/pictures-enough-rape-myths-hong-kong-protesters-march-sexual-violence/.
14 Catharine A. MacKinnon, "Feminism, Marxism, Method, and the State: Toward Feminist Jurisprudence", *The Standpoint Reader*: 169–79.
15 Ibid.
16 Tanya Hodgson, "September's Charity Spotlight: RainLily", *Liv: Hong Kong Wellness Magazine*, 14 September 2018. Retrieved from: https://liv-magazine

.com/septembers-charity-spotlight-rainlily/. The website of RainLily is in Chinese: https://rainlily.org.hk/. This NGO is called by this name because the general perception of a victim of sexual abuse is of being like a battered flower that has suffered the outrage of a tumultuous beating by a thunderstorm. The flower might be weak, but after the storms it continues to bloom; analogously, a victim of assault can recover and go on to flourish.

17 RainLily did not explain why they set the age at 14 on their website. In Hong Kong the age of consent is 16. In an unrelated study on Hong Kong teenagers, it is stated that girls complete their puberty development at age 14. Cf. Hui Wang, et al., "Age at Onset of Puberty and Adolescent Depression: 'Children of 1997' Birth Cohort", *Pediatrics* (May 2016): e20153231; DOI: https://doi.org/10.1542/peds.2015-3231.

18 Wang Yuke, "Sex Education—We Need to Adopt a More Open Approach", *China Daily*, 7 July 2019. Retrieved from: https://www.chinadailyhk.com/articles/186/12/10/1562514578891.html.

19 Shirley Zhao, "Eight in 10 Victims of Sexual Violence Know Their Attackers, and Many Are Afraid to Report the Incidents to Police, Hong Kong Study Shows", *South China Morning Post*, 31 May 2018. Retrieved from: https://www.scmp.com/news/hong-kong/hong-kong-law-and-crime/article/2148525/eight-10-victims-sexual-violence-know-their.

20 Blundy, "Hong Kong Police and Judicial System Accused of 'Victim Blaming Culture' as Rape Conviction Rate Falls: Campaigners Claim as Many as Nine in Ten Do Not Report Their Attackers".

21 Vivien Ng, "Ideology and Sexuality: Rape Laws in Qing China", *Journal of Asian Studies* 46.1 (1987): 57–72.

22 The Hong Kong Christian Council, a member of the World Council of Churches, was first initiated on 18 January 1954. It is a Protestant ecumenical organization and membership includes many mainline denominations, foreign mission churches, seminaries and also outreach organizations. But not all Christian churches, seminaries and organizations are members. Their website is in Chinese: https://www.hkcc.org.hk/acms/content.asp?site=hkccnew&op=showbycode&code=About.

23 Union of Catholic Asian News, "Hong Kong Protestant Leaders Accused of Sexual Harassment," *UCA News*, 28 June 2018. Retrieved from: https://www.ucanews.org/news/hong-kong-protestant-leaders-accused-of-sexual-harassment/82695; Lau Siu-fung, "#MeToo Complaints Rife in Hong Kong's Protestant Churches, as Victims Come Forward", *Radio Free Asia*, 25 June 2018 (trans. and ed. from Cantonese by Luisetta Mudie).

24 Ibid.

25 On the impact of the #MeToo movement in Hong Kong, see also Louisa Wong, "The Woman Leading #MeToo Movement in Hong Kong Says Movement 'Still Gaining Limited Attention'", *SBS Cantonese*, 21 March 2019. Retrieved from: https://www.sbs.com.au/language/english/the-woman-leading-metoo-in-hong-kong-says-movement-still-gaining-limited-attention.

26 Tim, "Reclaiming 'Slut' One Walk at a Time", *Plug*, 2 November 2017. Retrieved from: http://www.plug-magazine.com/slutwalk-2017/.

27 Evanna Gurung, "'It Won't Happen to Me': Activist Tackles Prejudice Against Sexual Violence Victims in Hong Kong", *South China Morning Post*, 25 August 2018. Retrieved from: https://www.scmp.com/news/hong-kong/community/article/2161141/it-wont-happen-me-activist-tackles-prejudice-against-sexual.

28 Ibid.
29 Catherine Lai, "SlutWalk Protesters to March Against Sexual Violence and Victim Blaming", *Hong Kong Free Press*, 13 November 2017. Retrieved from: https://www.hongkongfp.com/2017/11/13/slutwalk-protesters-march-sexual-violence-victim-blaming/.
30 Ibid. Lai cites the post in the *China Daily* that was taken down after overwhelming protests: "Chinese traditional values and conservative attitudes tend to safeguard women against inappropriate behaviour from members of the opposite gender". Such a claim associates Chinese traditional values with a reduction of incidents of rape. By implication, democratic or liberal values permit sexual violence to thrive. Such is not borne out by any evidence.
31 Josh Horowitz and Zheping Huang, "China's New Television Rules Ban Homosexuality, Drinking, and Vengeance", *Quartz*, 3 March 2016. Retrieved from: https://qz.com/630159/chinas-new-television-rules-ban-homosexuality-drinking-and-vengeance/.
32 Raquel Carvalho, "Thousands Gather at #MeToo Rally to Demand Hong Kong Police Answer Accusations of Sexual Violence Against Protesters", *South China Morning Post* 28 August 2019. Retrieved from: https://www.scmp.com/news/hong-kong/politics/article/3024789/thousands-gather-metoo-rally-demand-hong-kong-police-answer; Kris Cheng, "Hundreds of Masked Protesters Marched in Support of Hong Kong Student Who Accused Cop of Sexual Assault", *Hong Kong Free Press*, 11 October 2019. Retrieved from: https://www.hongkongfp.com/2019/10/11/hundreds-masked-protesters-march-support-hong-kong-student-accused-cop-sexual-assault/.
33 Lana Lam, "Risky Business: Sex Workers Walk a Blurred Line in the Streets of Wan Chai", *South China Morning Post* 9 November 2014; cited in Amnesty International, *Harmfully Isolated: Criminalizing Sex Work in Hong Kong* (London: Amnesty International, 2016), 15.
34 *Harmfully Isolated*, 15.
35 Haixia Ma and Alice Yuen Loke, "A Qualitative Study into Female Sex Workers' Experience of Stigma in the Health Care Setting in Hong Kong", *International Journal for Equity in Health* 175 (2019). Published 14 November 2019. Retrieved from: https://equityhealthj.biomedcentral.com/articles/10.1186/s12939-019-1084-1.
36 Ibid.
37 In January 2018, Hong Kong police officers arrested 99 foreign sex workers in a building in Mongkok. Clifford Lo, "Almost 100 Suspected Sex Workers Arrested in Hong Kong Anti-vice Crackdown", *South China Morning Post*, 28 January 2018. Retrieved from: https://www.scmp.com/news/hong-kong/law-crime/article/2131239/almost-100-suspected-sex-workers-arrested-hong-kong-anti.
38 Jun Pang, "Thinking Beyond the Stereotypes: The Diverse Experiences of Hong Kong Sex Workers", *Hong Kong Free Press*, 22 October 2017. Retrieved from: https://www.hongkongfp.com/2017/10/22/thinking-beyond-stereotypes-diverse-experiences-hong-kongs-sex-workers/.
39 I have used the figures provided by JJJ for the study here, simply for the fact that they have granted me permission to use them and because the reading exercises were conducted in JJJ premises. Some of these figures were also published in my earlier work. The statistics provided here concern the female sex workers in Hong Kong only.

40 Ipsen, 99–100.
41 "Midnight Blue", Global Network of Sex Work Projects, "Midnight Blue", NSWP (n.d.) Retrieved from: https://www.nswp.org/members/asia-and-the-pacific/midnight-blue.
42 Cf. their website at: https://teenskey.org/en/subpage.php?id=5.
43 "Columban Sisters Farewell Hong Kong: Peeking into Dark Corners", *Sunday Examiner* (2015). Published by the Bishop of the Roman Catholic Church Hong Kong. Retrieved from: http://sundayex.catholic.org.hk/node/2389.
44 For Action for REACH OUT's website, see: https://www.afro.org.hk/EN/mission.php.
45 Zi Teng does not make any claim to Christian affiliation and it does not discriminate against any volunteers or board members who are or who are not Christian. Zi Teng's website: http://www.ziteng.org.hk/eng/about-us.
46 Ibid. Access to Zi Teng's newsletters in English can be found here: http://www.ziteng.org.hk/eng/newsletter; and here is the link to their publications and other resources: http://www.ziteng.org.hk/eng/publication.
47 "Hong Kong Ordinances", Hong Kong Legal Institute (n.d.) Retrieved from: https://www.hklii.hk/eng/hk/legis/ord/200/
48 Cf. Viola Gaskell, "Inside Hong Kong's High-Rise Prostitution: Who's Really In-Charge?" *Daily Beast*, 17 October 2017 (updated 2 November 2017). Retrieved from: https://www.thedailybeast.com/inside-hong-kongs-high-rise-houses-of-prostitution-whos-really-in-charge. Gaskell correctly questions the feasibility of this law, as the sex workers' safety and survival precedes strict compliance to it.
49 Justin Heifeitz, "How Hong Kong's Patchy Sex Work Laws Enable Predatory Cops", *Vice*, 30 November 2016. Retrieved from: https://www.vice.com/en_uk/article/mvkpj8/how-hong-kongs-patchy-sex-work-laws-enable-predatory-cops.
50 Ibid.; *Harmfully Isolated*, 19–33.
51 The currency exchange rates are quoted as at 8 February 2020.
52 J.C.M. Li, "Violence Against Chinese Female Sex Workers in Hong Kong: From Understanding to Prevention", *International Journal of Offender Therapy and Comparative Criminology* 57 (2013): 621.
53 *Harmfully Isolated*, 10.

3 Sex workers read Tamar

Looking into the story of Tamar in Genesis 38 together with the Hong Kong sex workers made clear to me that today's interpretations—although often expressing sympathy for Tamar's predicament and even berating Judah—continue to be oblivious to the rape culture that the text depicts. Listening from the standpoint of the sex workers highlights this, while also showing how traditional interpretations stigmatise prostitutes in the biblical period as much as they do the sex workers of today. Beginning with a summary of the biblical narrative, then moving on to the interpretations of Chinese scholars and writers, whose works are often accessed by the Christian laity of Hong Kong today, the discussion then embarks on a "dialogue" or interface between the Hong Kong sex workers and contemporary Chinese and Western biblical scholarship.

3.1 The story in Genesis 38

Genesis 38 begins with Judah leaving his father and brothers and becoming acquainted with a certain man, an Adullamite (i.e. someone from the place called Adullam) called Hirah. Judah sees the daughter of a Canaanite named Shua and marries her. She bears him three sons: Er, Onan and Shelah. When the eldest son, Er, is of marriageable age, Judah finds him a wife, called Tamar. But YHWH, the deity, kills Er because he is wicked and Tamar is left a childless widow.

Judah then summons Onan—the next-oldest brother—to impregnate Tamar so as to leave a name—that is, a descendant—for his dead brother. (This practice is called the levirate law and is detailed elsewhere in the Bible, in Deuteronomy 25:5–10.) However, whenever Onan has intercourse with Tamar, he deliberately spills his semen on the ground, because he refuses to leave his brother a name. Instead, he wishes any offspring he might father to be known as his, not his (dead) brother Er's. YHWH is displeased by this deed and kills Onan as well. Judah, fearing that marrying Tamar might bring the same fate upon his youngest and only remaining son, Shelah, tells her to return to her father's house until Shelah comes of age. Tamar obeys but Judah does not summon her, even after years have passed.

Judah's wife dies, and after mourning for her, he goes with Hirah to visit the sheepshearers at Timnah. Tamar learns of Judah's itinerary and takes matters into her own hands. She removes her widow's clothes, conceals her identity with a veil, and waits for him at the gate of Enaim, which leads to Timnah. When Judah sees her, he thinks she is a prostitute and asks if he might solicit her services. They strike a deal. He promises to pay her with a lamb later, but she asks for the pledge of his seal, cord and staff—which are his identity markers—and he agrees immediately. They have intercourse. Once the deed is done, Tamar returns home and puts on her widow's clothes again. Tamar conceives.

Judah then sends Hirah with the promised lamb to look for the woman, so that he may pay her and reclaim his pledges. Hirah asks the townspeople the whereabouts of the *qdsh* (sometimes translated "cult prostitute" or "shrine prostitute") by the roadside, but they tell him that there is no *qdsh* in their town. So Hirah returns and reports back to Judah. Judah decides not to pursue the matter for fear of becoming a laughingstock and resolves to relinquish his pledges. He believes, in matters of conscience, he has attempted to keep his word.

Three months later, Judah is told that Tamar is pregnant. He immediately calls for her to be burned alive. But when she is brought out, she shows the pledges of the man who impregnated her. Judah acknowledges them as his and proclaims Tamar to be more righteous than he. He brings her back into his household, but does not have intercourse with her again. Tamar gives birth to twins and they are acknowledged to be Judah's sons.

3.2 Hong Kong Christian interpretations

This section will now look at how Chinese scholars and writers interpret this story. For this purpose, two popular Chinese commentaries and some pieces of devotional literature suffice: the first is a short commentary on the book of Genesis by Andrew Chiu,[1] who attempts to relate the biblical narrative to Chinese culture wherever a possibility arises; and the second is a more elaborate work on Genesis by Andrew P.C. Kwong that comes in five volumes.[2] There are also two very short excerpts about Tamar which appear in volumes 2 and 3 of a popular *Daily Devotional Book for Women*, written by various Chinese Christian scholars.[3] For my purposes here, I focus on the following key events: 1) 38:11, where Tamar is told to return home; 2) 38:14 and 18, where Tamar is the subject of all the verbs, where it states Tamar has conceived; 3) 38:20–3, Hirah's use of *qdsh* when searching for Tamar; and 4) 38:24–5, where Tamar's pregnancy is discovered. These passages recount what is done to Tamar and what she does. Chinese Christian communities find it difficult to appreciate that YHWH allows Tamar to conceive under such circumstances, so it becomes crucial for the authors of these works to provide a "comfortable" explanation.

3.2.1 Tamar is to return home in Gen 38:11

> "Then Judah said to his daughter-in-law Tamar, 'Stay as a widow in your father's house until my son Shelah grows up'—for he thought, 'He too might die like his brothers'. So Tamar went to live in her father's house".

Chiu takes great pains to draw inferences from the text and to relate these to Chinese culture. For example, in relation to Judah's soliloquy (v.11b), where his fear of losing Shelah if he gives him to Tamar functions as a justification to send her back to her father's house, Chiu cites the Chinese superstition known as 克夫 *kefu*.[4] The word 克 *ke* means "to stifle", and 夫 *fu* refers to "husband". This word denotes a woman who is believed to have stifled the life and good prospects of her husband, thereby causing his untimely death. Chiu presents Judah's actions as understandable in the light of such a superstition, and as forgivable in Chinese cultural terms also. Hence, he blames *Tamar* rather than YHWH for Er's death.

For his part, Kwong simply exegetes the text, explaining that in the case of a childless marriage where the husband has died, the woman usually returns to her father's house and is free to remarry if her father so arranges.[5] In Kwong's view, the fact that Judah mentions Shelah in this instruction indicates that the levirate law is still binding after Onan's death, and Tamar therefore cannot remarry or have sexual relations with anyone else. Kwong continues that Judah is being deceitful because he has no intention of giving Shelah to Tamar. Kwong also admires the unquestioning obedience of Tamar. Of the devotional commentaries, DDW2 expresses the view that Tamar must have felt hopeless and extremely hurt by the order to return home.[6] Both DDW2 and DDW3 opine that the waiting period strengthened Tamar and made her resolved to take action for herself.[7] Comparatively speaking, the two devotional materials give more thought to Tamar as a person and subject than Chiu or Kwong.

3.2.2 Tamar's actions in 38:14 and her conception in 38:18

> "So she took off her widow's garb, covered her face with a veil, and wrapping herself up, sat down at the entrance to Enaim, which is on the road to Timnah; for she saw that Shelah was grown up, yet she had not been given to him as wife".

> "And he said, 'What pledge shall I give you?' She replied, 'Your seal and cord, and the staff which you carry'. So he gave them to her and slept with her, and she conceived by him".

Chiu spills much ink over the episode of Tamar deceiving Judah, explaining why it is possible Judah does not recognise her.[8] He cites vv.14–15, which say she covered her whole body and "put on the veil", and also mentions that they have not met for a very long time. Moreover, he stresses, Tamar makes efforts not to be recognised. Chiu adds that Judah's wife has been dead for some time and he has passed the mourning period; so, it is natural for Judah to have bodily needs. Chiu adds an explanation that the word *znh* in the Hebrew Bible refers to a prostitute, whose services could be called on at any time.[9] Kwong, on the other hand, does not rationalise on Judah's behalf. He simply points out that Judah seems to be rather lustful right from the beginning of the story. Here, when Judah sees Shua's daughter, he decides to marry her; and now, at this encounter with a woman at the city gate, he assumes that she must be a prostitute.[10] Kwong suggests that the mention of Tamar's change of clothes in v.14 is important here, for he goes on to draw comparisons between Tamar's veil used to deceive Judah and Judah and Joseph's brothers using a blood-stained coat to deceive Jacob. In these deceptions, "clothes", "sheep" and "recognition" are common elements.[11]

Chiu makes an attempt to justify Tamar's actions by referring to the biblical author's comment about conception (38:18). He rationalises that in ancient Israel, the principles of the Law supercede ethics. Thus, Tamar's actions of deception and impersonating a prostitute can be justified in the light of the Law (in particular Deuteronomy 25:5–10). Chiu reasons that since Judah will not give Shelah to Tamar, then Judah himself is actually the kinsman nearest to her deceased husband. Consequently, her actions, while not complying with levirate law, can be justified.[12] Kwong, on the other hand, argues for the straightforward legality of Tamar's actions as complying with levirate customs, citing Hittite Law §193 and the example of Ruth—where "kin" is not limited to "brothers" (of a husband) as in Deuteronomy 25:5–10, but to the closest male kin.[13]

3.2.3 Hirah's search for the qdsh in Gen 38:20–23

> "*Judah sent the kid by his friend the Adullamite, to redeem the pledge from the woman; but he could not find her. He inquired of the people of that town, 'Where is the cult prostitute, the one at Enaim, by the road?' But they said, 'There has been no prostitute here'. So he returned to Judah and said, 'I could not find her; moreover, the townspeople said: There has been no prostitute here'. Judah said, 'Let her keep them, lest we become a laughingstock. I did send her this kid, but you did not find her'".*

Concerning the episode of Judah's friend Hirah searching for the woman that Judah encountered, Chiu interprets the word *qdsh* ("cult prostitute") to refer to one of the women who work at the temple, or, in some places, female priests.[14] These women have to be virgins when they enter the temples, and their work duties are to serve the devotees and at times offer their bodies to them. He considers that this is one of the most disgusting and degenerate customs of the Canaanites. He goes on to construe that during ancient times, people visited *qdshym* (the plural of *qdsh*) rather than local prostitutes. This explains why, should the townsfolk discover Judah had engaged a prostitute, he would become a target of mockery.

Kwong explains that *qdsh* refers to a woman who becomes a prostitute in the temple, because some Canaanite religions practised a custom where a woman had to sell her body at least once in her life so that she might become fertile.[15] Kwong argues strongly against interpreting Tamar as either being or pretending to be a *qdsh*. He reasons that Hirah's use of *qdsh* functions as a euphemism, out of courtesy to the local townsfolk— that is, so as not to imply that their town is hosting common prostitutes. The second reason Kwong offers is that use of the word *qdsh* maintains respect for Judah: in other words, he had engaged a cult prostitute like the people there often did, and not an ordinary one, which might make him a laughingstock. Judah and Hirah both, therefore, consider soliciting a prostitute a shameful thing, and neither wants to mention to anyone that Judah has done so.

3.2.4 Judah sentences Tamar to death in Gen 38:24–25

> "*About three months later, Judah was told, 'Your daughter-in-law Tamar has played the harlot (from* znh*); in fact, she is with child by harlotry (from* znh*)'. 'Bring her out', said Judah, 'and let her be burned'. As she was being brought out, she sent this message to her father-in-law, 'I am with child by the man to whom these belong'. And she added, 'Examine these, whose seal and cord and staff are these?'"*

Words from *znh* appear again in v.24, where Judah is told Tamar is pregnant because she has prostituted herself. Both Chiu and Kwong point out that Tamar needs to let Judah know what has really happened, and an informer does the job.[16] Kwong adds that someone must have felt sympathy for Tamar and wants to see justice done. However, Judah's first reaction is to have Tamar dragged out (from her home?) to burn her alive (v.25). Chiu explains that this is another custom of that time, where adultery is punished in this way, often including both the offending male and female.[17] Kwong observes that Judah's summons for Tamar to be killed indicates just how much he wants to get rid of her.[18]

Chiu explains that Tamar's presentation of the pledges is proof that Tamar has not acted like a prostitute as the rumour suggested. She wants justice.[19] Both commentators commend Judah for his confession. For Chiu, Judah upholds Tamar over himself; he acquits her of his earlier death sentence; and he also admits his wrongdoing against her.[20] At this point, Chiu is also eager to warn that what has taken place is incest and a severe crime in Chinese culture.[21] He comments that should such a thing ever occur in a Chinese context, Tamar would not have been let off lightly. He thinks that this is a special case in ancient Israel where fulfilling the principle of the Law supercedes that of ethics. He argues that since Judah withholds Shelah from Tamar, Judah remains the only person to impregnate Tamar under the levirate law. Chiu does not explicate further his notion of "ethics" and his views on incest in the biblical period, nor cite other biblical references. Kwong, following most scholars, believes that the biblical author is portraying a transformed Judah— from the beginning of the narrative up to this point, Judah has become more compassionate.[22] He thus takes this moment as the climax of the story, in which Judah is the focus, i.e. what Judah was before, and what he has now become.

3.2.5 *General summary of Hong Kong Christian interpretations*

Kwong seems to be more sympathetic to Tamar than Chiu, for he devotes a good paragraph to praising Tamar's integrity. Despite her Canaanite identity, she obeys the Law (Torah) and endures the bullying of Judah and his sons. She uses her intelligence and courage to overcome her situation and receives justice. Nonetheless, Kwong keeps referring to Tamar's actions as "unscrupulous", warning Christians not to replicate her deed of deception and her pretence of being a prostitute.[23] Kwong interprets this story in its larger framework as a polemic against the Canaanites. Hence, Judah leaving his family, becoming acquainted with his Canaanite friend, and marrying a Canaanite wife, are taken to be indications of degeneration. Seen in this light, Tamar's actions are those of a gentile and Judah's wickedness can be blamed on the Canaanites for corrupting him. He concludes that this story reinforces the principle of retribution: hence, Judah is deceived and humiliated by Tamar on account of what he did to her first.

DDW2 presents the story of Tamar in a similar way: suggesting the crux is Judah's ethical Israelite traditions confronting abominable Canaanite customs and practices. DDW2 explains further that this must be the reason why YHWH kills both Er and Onan, for they have become evil, just like the Canaanites. However, Canaanite Tamar is declared more worthy than Judah and his sons. DDW2 explains it is necessary for her to be impregnated by Judah's family in order to restore her fate. The author of DDW2 concludes that despite the difficulties life presents, one must remain optimistic, because God will present an opportunity. DDW2 offers the following questions for reflection: "Tamar was intimate with several men; have you had similar experiences and treatment? Do you see God opening a door for you?" DDW3 gives a shorter description of the story, emphasising the humiliation Tamar undergoes when she is sent home to wait for so long without any prospect of having a child; and states that Tamar pretends to be a temple prostitute so as to seduce Judah and become pregnant. The reflection on the passage encourages any woman who might be at rock bottom because of humiliation that they can have hope that God will help them receive justice. Clearly, since the freely available Chinese commentaries take the Canaanite culture to be blameworthy for influencing Israel, the two devotional materials do likewise. Hence there is a conscious effort to differentiate between what constitutes influences that are "worldly" or "spiritual". The Chinese Christian must denounce the earlier and embrace the latter. So, while there is some sympathy for Tamar, Tamar has not conscientiously denounced her Canaanite roots. Hence, pejorative statements are made about Tamar by DDW2, accusing her of having sexual relations with "several men" instead of saying "three", and also not highlighting Tamar's patience, initiative and courage in getting herself out of her dire circumstances, rather than passively waiting any longer and hoping for Judah's deity to act on her behalf.

3.3 The sex workers' standpoint

In this section, it becomes apparent that the sex workers' standpoint offers an entirely new perspective on the story of Judah and Tamar. I shall first present the sex workers' views on why they think v.9 is indicative of rape culture; secondly, why v.14 is regarded as the climax of the story instead of v.26; and thirdly, what they think of the episode of Hirah using the term *qdsh*. Their insights highlight how both the biblical narrative and common interpretations of it promote rape culture and the stigmatization of sex workers.

When the story in Genesis 38 was presented to them, all the sex workers were instantly drawn to the character of Tamar. They all expressed strong negative opinions towards laws such as the levirate decree, commenting that such laws benefit the male in every way, while women are treated as commodities. In their view, most women, including Tamar, do not know their options, hence they simply believe and accept what their men decide to be their fate. They all felt sorry for Tamar.

3.3.1 Gen 38:9 is a rape text

> "But Onan, knowing that the seed would not count as his, let it go to waste whenever he joined with his brother's wife, so as not to provide offspring for his brother".

After the levirate custom was explained, one sex worker pointed out that v.9 constitutes an account of Onan's rape of Tamar. She reasoned that Tamar's agreement to have sexual intercourse was so that she could become pregnant; but since Onan does not keep his part of the agreement, what he does amounts to rape. Before sex workers perform any services, their clients discuss what they would like and a price is negotiated according to the sex workers' price list.[24] Whenever a client suddenly deviates from the original agreement during the course of the service, it amounts to a breach of agreement and, in some cases, rape. The reason is that consent is given only to a specified sexual act/s not to any other or additional act/s. In Chapter 2 (2.1), according to the rape law, the specificity of a woman's consent is very important both before and at the time of sexual intercourse. Hence, in circumstances that the sex workers encounter, their consent is granted only for what was earlier agreed, and not for anything else. Agreeing to "sex" does not equate agreeing to "everything sexual". If the sex workers can, they will stop the service immediately and demand the client compensate them or leave, but on many occasions, they find themselves in a vulnerable position or threatened into complying. This makes them feel afraid and angry, but there is no one who can right the wrongs they suffer. The law does not usually protect the rights of a sex worker in situations such as these, so sex workers simply send out warnings to other sisters about a particular client.

Tamar negotiating with Judah in vv.16b–18 is an example of what a transaction for sexual services looks like. In fact, the sex workers were quick to commend Judah for his integrity in honouring the promise he made to the woman he believed to be a prostitute. Judah sends Hirah to look for her with the agreed payment. The sex workers noted that many who are new to the industry are tricked by a client's promises—e.g. the client leaves a passport or identity document as a guarantee of later payment, but then fails to return, since the documents are fake. The sex workers felt that Judah was a better businessman than family man. That is why he treats the prostitute better than Tamar, his daughter-in-law. They admitted that from their experience, most businessmen treat them fairly and with respect, because businessmen tend to handle the transaction for sex like other deals, as a matter of honour.

The sex workers therefore felt Tamar was both naïve and a victim of rape by Onan. A few expressed concerns about the duration of the sexual abuse before her assailant was struck dead. In their view YHWH was waiting for Onan to come around to fulfilling his duty, rather than considering Tamar's victimization and humiliation. Perhaps YHWH struck Onan dead only because Onan showed no remorse and became more determined to defy the Law? Onan was not struck dead, however, because of any compassion for Tamar on YHWH's part.

No commentator I found calls the action of Onan rape. The commentaries call it deception only, or a dishonouring of the Law and of Tamar and Judah's family. That is given as the reason why YHWH strikes Onan dead. Even Kwong, who has no kind words for this Israelite family, does not call Onan's action rape; nor do DDW2 and 3, which use the word "humiliate" instead.

Interestingly, Gerald Janzen offers an interesting interpretation of Tamar in this regard: he juxtaposes the way Tamar is deceived and treated as a prostitute three times by Judah and his sons, with the three times Tamar is in fact, "the holy one" (the literal meaning of *qdsh*).[25] Perhaps Janzen is attempting to make a literary connection between the words *znh* and *qdsh*; and perhaps he believes he has elevated Tamar above Judah and his sons. Again, this interpretation is problematic. First, the text does not comment on Er's sins, apart from the fact they deserve YHWH's punishment by death, so it is hard to pinpoint how he has mistreated Tamar, if indeed he has. Second, to polarise prostitute (*znh*) against "the holy one" (*qdsh*), two words which occur in parallel in other places in the Hebrew Bible, indicating their near-synonymous meaning, is to stigmatise one (i.e. prostitutes and, by extension, the sex workers of today). On the other hand, the *qdsh* is, by implication, someone who might have been in the ancient Near East regarded as respectable. But to juxtapose these two words means that poor treatment of a *znh*, including the misdeeds of Judah and his son Onan against Tamar, are rendered justifiable. By extension, bad treatment of sex workers, including deceiving them, breaking an arrangement and even raping them, or standing by when they are sentenced to death, is also implicitly condoned—because they are "only prostitutes". Janzen proposes that Tamar's deception has a holy purpose but his argument offers little in terms of regard for sex workers and their rights.

3.3.2 Gen 38:14 is the climax of the story

The sex workers were all drawn to v.14 (cited above) and kept returning to it. In the end, they decided v.14 is the key verse of the whole story. I shall present their insights below in three stages: 1) What Tamar sees; 2) what Tamar decides to do; and 3) what Tamar overcomes.

3.3.2.1 What Tamar sees

The sex workers were eager to point out that Tamar finally "sees" her situation. They linked what she "sees" to vv.11ff. After all the years of waiting for the order to return, Tamar realises Judah has no intention of keeping his word and fulfilling the levirate law even though he had earlier enforced it. The sex workers commented that Judah is contradictory in his observance of the Law. If he has no intention of keeping the levirate law, he should issue a divorce bill to Tamar, not make her observe a perpetual widowhood.

The sex workers were also keen to point out that they could identify with Tamar's shame whenever her townsfolk might ask her why she is doubly widowed and why Judah has not asked her home. Added to that, she cannot live like an ordinary woman, for she has to wear her mourning widow garments all the time. Furthermore, they asked, how long can Tamar wait? After all, she has a biological clock that is ticking. The shame of being sent home to observe her widowhood, condemned to childlessness by her in-laws, must be a source of unbearable emotional pain and distress for Tamar. The sex workers pointed out that Judah's family treats Tamar like a non-human: she is raped by Onan, and then tortured psychologically by Judah because he is allegedly observing YHWH's levirate law.

Some of the sex workers also said Onan should have offered Tamar the bill of divorce since he had no intention to fulfil the levirate duty, as Kwong also mentions.[26] Similarly, Judah could have instructed Shelah to do so as well, so that arrangements could have been made for Tamar to remarry. Hence, Judah's crime against Tamar escalates. Nevertheless, commentators like Chiu and others continue to justify Judah by explaining that his soliloquy in v.11 is understandable to everyone who has children![27]

The sex workers protested that anyone who justifies Judah's words in v.11 demonstrates inhumanity to their daughters. They argued that if Tamar were Judah's daughter, this evil deed would not have happened. The sex workers were, however, unaware of the stories in Genesis 19 and Judges 19–21, where fathers betray their daughters, offering them up for gang rape (Genesis 19:8; Judges 19:24).[28] They did not press further why Tamar's father does not do something to help his daughter.

Another thing that Tamar "sees" is her opportunity. Just as most commentators take the death of Judah's wife and the end of Judah's period of mourning, in conjunction with his taking a journey to be with his sheepshearers (perhaps to drink and carouse), as a signal and justification for Judah's "need" for a prostitute, so does Tamar. The sex workers also commented that the story is presented to Judah's advantage, with double standards applied to Tamar. His thoughts and actions can be "justified" and he is considered "honourable", because he makes a confession (v.26). Thus, after his wife has been dead for a while and he has completed his mourning, he can be morally excused for having sexual "needs" and engaging a prostitute—but this is not the case for Tamar. Hence, in v.24, when Judah hears Tamar is pregnant, she is accused of "prostitution" and must be punished by death! There is no allowance made for *her* sexual needs.

The sex workers sighed: the Bible and society consider it is okay for a patriarch, a man of status, to solicit prostitutes, because of his sexual needs and financial means, but the prostitutes whom the patriarch solicits are condemned and a woman who has sex outside of a legalised bond is sentenced to death. At the same time, many commentators fail to point out Tamar's needs, just like Judah, who gives no thought to them. His needs make sense; they are justified and everyone can account for them, but her needs—to conceive and become a mother, to have her body honoured and respected—are abused and dismissed. As the sex workers pointed out, the patriarch's bodily needs become important above all other considerations. Here we have the root of the problem of rape culture: men's needs are considered more important than women's needs. Women's bodies must be regulated according to men's urgencies and male initiation. Women's bodies exist to fulfil men's needs. The body of Judah's wife has died—has ceased to perform its sexual function in meeting Judah's needs—and it is, therefore, understandable that he has desires and so his actions are excused and pardoned. The woman's reaction to this need must be one of compliance, but if she is a prostitute, she is maligned. Men's needs and their abusive conduct are excusable, understood and even respected; women's needs are problematic and called to account. When she succumbs to a man's sexual advances, regardless of the circumstances, the woman in this story is called a "whore" who has committed "whoredom" and who deserves to be punished. No questions are asked and no investigation is made when Tamar is found to be pregnant (was she raped? Was she treated fairly by her in-laws?); instead, she is immediately condemned to being burned to death.

Indeed, one can find modern commentators spreading the same injustices. Chiu's misogynistic exegesis is no different from those of some of the best-known Western commentaries. It is one thing to explain what the text signifies; it is another not to point out the injustice occurring here and to continue to minimise and silence Tamar's suffering. Moreover, if we do not point out the problems of the narrative and of these interpretations, we simply resign to such treatment of women's bodies being "natural" and pardonable. Consequently, rape culture becomes natural and pardonable too.

Most of the sex workers imagined Tamar might have had thoughts of seducing Judah earlier whenever he visited her hometown for business in previous years, but because Tamar is moral and obedient, she refused to seize these opportunities. She would not hurt and disrespect her mother-in-law in this way. It is at this point, since her mother-in-law is now out of the picture, Tamar acts.

In summary, the sex workers read what Tamar "saw" as a flashback to the events that have led to where she is in v.14. She recognises the injustices committed against her body and against her dignity as a person—and by Judah in particular, who thinks he has conveniently disposed of her. She also "sees" her opportunity and so decides to take action. In the commentaries, most scholars highlight the name of the place where Tamar sits in wait for Judah: the gate of Enaim means "Open Eyes".[29] But whereas Tamar recognises her injustice, Judah, like most commentators, does *not* recognise her, but only sees what his body wants: a prostitute.

3.3.2.2 What Tamar does to seduce Judah

One of the sex workers drew attention to Tamar's garments. She commented insightfully that the widow's garments that Judah ordered Tamar to wear have been her prison, a prolonged prison under Judah's jurisdiction. For Tamar's plot to succeed, she has to remove her widow's garments and exchange them for the veil. The sex worker felt this was the most difficult thing Tamar had to do. The rest of the sex workers were enlightened by this insight and started to contribute eagerly, sharing their own experiences.

The sex workers admitted that they could identify with Tamar's difficulty in removing her widow's garments, because they had had similar experiences. They talked about how they struggled to remove their clothes the first time they performed sex work. It took them ages, they recalled, to remove their clothes to serve their very first clients. Some remembered how their clients grew impatient with them, while a few said they had had nicer clients who were extremely kind and waited until they felt ready (one shared she needed more than 30 minutes). They recounted they kept unbuttoning and buttoning up their clothes many times before they finally gave in.

They imagined Tamar struggling a great deal to "put off the widow's garments" and "put on the veil". They believed that like them, Tamar must have "put off" and "put on" her garments many times before finally walking out into the street. Although the widow's garment is her prison, it has also defined her for a long time, and it is how the world is used to identifying her. While Tamar possibly hates it, she has no doubt become accustomed to it and she probably even feels comfortable and secure in it. But what she "sees" inspires her courage to "put on the veil". She is a widowed daughter-in-law in those garments and what she is about to do will defy all the familial and societal expectations that come with the garment. How will her family, Judah's family, and the rest of the world react to what she is about to do?

Next, the sex workers felt strongly that the narrator is painting too naïve a scenario for the reader, as if the street contains only Tamar in her veil and Judah, with no one else around. If Tamar intends the passerby to perceive her as a prostitute, one just like other prostitutes who ply their trade at the city gate, then she must have to chase off other potential clients. And because she refuses to concede to their demands, she will be at risk of harassment and even rape and abuse. Furthermore, she might even be challenged or questioned by the other prostitutes already there. Even assuming Tamar does not pretend to be a prostitute, but is just sitting there, she is exposed to the same element of threat. The sex workers thought it would be hard for Tamar to simply "target" Judah. It is hard to imagine Tamar doing so without any obstacle in the real world.

One of the sex workers shared her own experience of getting lost on the way to a small hotel to serve a client. She was not dressed provocatively, but in plain office attire with sunglasses, and it was around 3pm on a spring afternoon. There were some construction workers along the road, and when they saw her walking back and forth looking for the street number, they started to whistle at her and make loud comments about her appearance. They jeered that she did not look like an office worker, but like a sex worker trying to seduce them, because she kept pacing back and forth. She was terrified at first, but finally told herself they had no right to make comments about her clothing or to threaten her. She ignored them completely, and thankfully, not long after, found the small entrance to the hotel. She said in streets like these, men assert their dominance by being sexist and by threatening women's spaces. They enjoy making women feel afraid, and overtly expressing their objectification of women's bodies. The problem is: in our society and culture, there is no attempt by the law to curb such behaviour. Women, on the other hand, are taught by family and peers to avoid or run away from places where such men behave in ways like these. It is ridiculous that even in public locations, women must regulate their bodies to accommodate men. Hence, this sex worker believed Tamar must have had to face similar challenges, especially when walking alone in her veil to the city gate, and sitting there waiting for Judah. Such a public place in ancient times is likely to have been the preserve and territory of men, as well as a place where prostitutes hung out. Tamar, disguised as she is as a sex worker, is thus exposed to the possibility of harassment and rape.

The sex workers had much to say about Tamar's veil. They admitted they, likewise, "put on a veil". All the advertisements outside their doors, online and in other media, only have pictures of their bodies, not their faces. Many have families and relatives who do not know they are sex workers. The need to conceal their faces and their true identities is a real issue for them. They all know this veil, which they put on when at work. At the same time, and just like Tamar, this veil offers them a new lease of life from the former one which imprisoned them. Yet having to put on the veil ushers in new "fears".

They explained what these fears are, and stated they are all real and still affect them today in one way or another: social expectations of family, loved ones, neighbours and society in general. Society has labelled sex workers as morally deficient or dubious, and sex work as a degradation of selfhood. However, these labels do not help sex workers in overcoming the very problems that compel them to become sex workers in the first place. Just as Tamar experiences, the very power that could free her closes its fists against her. Tamar grows tired of her fears and how the rest of the world might judge her. The sex workers said that to survive in this world, women have to fight for themselves, because no one else will fight for them. All the men in their lives had failed them, had failed to protect them and their children. For their own sakes and for a better life for their children, they had to conquer fear and do what they could for themselves—just like Tamar. The journey of this awakening demands courage and inner strength in order to overcome life threats, social marginalization and possible excommunication from one's community towards a redefinition of one's self-esteem. The first sex worker, who had brought our attention to the widow's garment, concluded that in v.14 Tamar's body becomes one with their sex worker bodies. They had all, like Tamar, lived through experiences of fear and taking risks for the sake of their children, or, in Tamar's case, for the children yet to be born. The others concurred.

Commentators argue over whether the veil is a costume or signifier for prostitutes in the biblical period.[30] Tammi Schneider debunks any suggestion that widows at that time wore an "identifiable garb", and argues that veils were common accessories for women, not the mark of prostitutes in particular. Tamar, she argues, uses the veil to conceal her identity—nothing more.[31] The other interpretation, as mentioned earlier, is to compare the garment to that of the Joseph narratives. Overall, these scholars offer no deeper insights than the sex workers. While the sex workers did not argue the veil is *the* identifiable garment for prostitutes in the biblical period, they nevertheless took its function to be that of concealment, both literally and also symbolically, in terms of reflecting their own concealment and "fears".

None of the works I have consulted consider v.14 to be the climax of the story, with all claiming the later verses 38:20–5 as the climax (see below). Schneider does give space to exegete and interpret v.14. For the sex workers, this verse is crucial because the plot hinges upon it, i.e. for Tamar "to see" and hence succeed. I suppose this depends somewhat on whether we think the true protagonist is Judah or Tamar. Although Judah seems to praise Tamar, it is still from his standpoint: "she is more in the right than I" (38:26). In other words, the point is how much *he* has changed or is willing to change to be able to say this. Hence, the honour still goes to him. He is evaluating things that have happened from his standpoint. Kwong's conclusion about the narrative is correct only if one thinks v.26 is the key to the story, which is about how Judah has changed from being selfish and deceiving into a more sympathetic and humble man. Because the sex workers appreciate the story of Tamar as their story, they see the true protagonist as Tamar, and therefore, the key to the whole narrative lies in Tamar's awakening. From this vantage point, the decisive moment is the one in which she decides to act and to change her life. This definitive moment comes in v.14, after which the other events fall into place, with the resolution occurring in vv.20–5.

Above all, the sex workers offer us an insight into what Tamar possibly experiences: her struggle before she embarks on her mission. Gordon Wenham interprets the occurrences of the waw-consecutive verbs in v.14 to mean that "she suddenly races into rapid, purposeful action... in verse 14 she quickly takes off, covers, wraps herself, sits down at the strategic location".[32] Perhaps the male narrator and Wenham are eager to get to the seduction and sex scene, and it requires our sex workers to highlight the fact that these actions are by no means hasty or taken without due consideration.

As mentioned above, all the scholarship claims the climax of the story to be Genesis 38:26, where Judah proclaims Tamar is more righteous than he is. Jione Havea argues that Judah only admits he is the one who has impregnated Tamar, but does not admit to his injustice against her.[33] Many, like Claus Westermann, Derek Kidner and John Hartley, do not fail to mention that Judah is "honourable" because he admits to his fault.[34] It is now much clearer that when suggesting the climax is at v.26, it becomes Judah's story—it is about Judah, his oversight, his wrong and his realization and repentance. Yet according to the sex workers, this is Tamar's story and their story—of how society imposes patriarchal structures against their wishes, of their hardships, their struggles and their overcoming challenges. They all felt that because Tamar has "awakened", even if she had failed to conceive at this first attempt, she will try again, perhaps by other means, but she will do everything necessary to fight for her own survival.

3.3.3 *Hirah's use of* qdsh

It was explained to the sex workers that in the context of the ancient Near East, the term *qdsh* is understood as a female religious figure whose sexual roles are not clear, and that the Bible usually translates the word as "temple prostitute" or similar. They were asked what they thought of this usage when Judah's friend is unable to find the sex worker that Judah has described to him.

3.3.3.1 qdsh *means an outsider*

Several sex workers suspected that the story's intention was to praise Judah. They thus felt the use of *qdsh* is to spare Judah embarrassment in that he does not solicit an ordinary prostitute, but a special religious one. This interpretation seems to be a common one even among biblical scholars. The notion that *qdsh* might be a more polite term for prostitute, or a reference to an elite prostitute, is espoused by Kwong and others. This interpretation might go some way towards saving face for Judah. Others, such as Victor Hamilton, following Phyllis Bird, explain that Hirah interprets Judah's use of *znh* to be "plain" speech and so when Hirah relates to the people in that town, he uses *qdsh* because it is "polite" speech.³⁵

A few sex workers disagreed that *qdsh* in any way "elevates" Judah's choice of prostitute. They reasoned that if *qdsh* denotes service to a foreign god, then what Judah does would be particularly offensive to Judah's god YHWH, who might strike Judah dead, too. While some thought that *qdsh* might just be a more "respectable" or polite term for a prostitute, others suggested perhaps it was another way of affirming that those who do sex work cannot also be YHWH worshippers. They compared this with Christians who expressed horror at learning that there are sex workers who are also Christians. Such Christians assume that sex workers must be non-Christians. Similarly, they said Christians sometimes assume that male Christians do not solicit sex workers and that when they do, other Christians consider them non-Christians. Basically, what the sex workers meant was that calling someone *qdsh* identifies them as an outsider, a non-Israelite.

The new insight is that the term *qdsh* is not necessarily used here because Hirah is adjusting terminology for the sake of preserving Judah's reputation. Instead, the term might be reiterating the notion that the female concerned is not or cannot be an Israelite. This may be more for the sake of the readers than for the movement of the plot. But for the sex workers this was perceived as yet another tool to marginalise them: in contemporary contexts, such a strategy might signify that they are not considered worthy of inclusion, of being Christian, for example.

Contrary to the many scholars accusing Tamar of acting like a *qdsh*, the sex workers' deduction is that Judah is taking a risk in approaching a woman who appears to be a temple prostitute: YHWH could have struck him dead! Nonetheless, we find Chinese commentaries on this text saying that Tamar is a practising *qdsh*.³⁶ These commentators believe she must be, because she is a Canaanite, and Canaanite religious practices teach women to do such things. These works of commentary create a polemic between Canaanite and Israelite culture, with one portrayed as debased beyond reason, deserving punishment, and the other as exalted and pure. Although Kwong argues against taking Tamar as a *qdsh*, he still draws on the polemic between Israel and Canaan throughout his interpretation. While Tamar is to be pitied, Kwong believes she is still deceptive and unscrupulous—just as one might expect from a Canaanite.³⁷ This polemical and discriminatory interpretation is at the root of marginalization and stigmatization, which the sex workers pointed out by drawing an analogy with the way Christians regard sex workers today: as people who can not be part of the Christian community.

3.3.3.2 *Tamar is neither a* qdsh *nor a prostitute*

The sex workers also opined Hirah was being silly, because he should have been looking for a prostitute, and not a *qdsh*. One of them suggested that the biblical author must have left out a part where Hirah has already sought out the prostitutes and cannot find Tamar among them. So, he thinks, "perhaps she's a *qdsh*"—and that is why he goes to ask the people of the place. The reason here, as one sex worker argued, is that men know where to look for prostitutes, and prostitutes in turn know their sisters. By comparison, a practising religious female might be more elusive than a prostitute. As they discussed the matter further, all of them agreed in the end, regardless of whether the term was correct or not, that neither Hirah nor the commoners would ever discover that the woman is actually Tamar, because she is neither a "prostitute" nor a *qdsh*.

Interestingly, the sex workers' insights about the search for Tamar were ingenious. First, no scholar had thought about the possibility that Hirah might have already failed in his attempt to find the woman in the most likely places. This interpretation also takes seriously the fact that Hirah is a local and that sending him on this search among his people makes sense. In addition, if indeed it is the occasion for sheep shearing, many more men would be at the city gate. Tamar is not alone. There must be other prostitutes there also soliciting clients, given the occasion. It is possible many people, including the local prostitutes, see a woman like Tamar but cannot identify her. Hence, Tamar is not merely veiling herself so that Judah will not recognise her, but is veiling herself from the locals as well. No one there knows who this woman is, and they are too busy to find out. It would not make sense for there to be no other prostitutes on the evening of a public hubbub like this.

Drawing from the sex workers' insights, I suggest that one need not interpret the use of *qdsh* in relation to Judah fearing being made a laughingstock. It is more likely that the conclusion may have been that if neither the prostitute nor the *qdsh* could be found, then Judah has been deceived by a wandering adulteress. That will make him a laughingstock and it might also bring her cuckolded husband out after Judah's blood! Alternatively, Judah may have encountered a ghost, or phantom! Revelation of such would also make him a laughingstock.

3.4 Chapter summary

In this chapter, I compared the interpretations from predominantly Chinese but also some Western scholarship with those of the Hong Kong sex workers. From their standpoints, the sex workers made the following observations: 1) 38:9 is a rape text; 2) 38:14 is the climax of the story; and 3) the use of *qdsh* is a literary device to marginalise Tamar, by asserting that her actions are not those of an Israelite. In a number of ways, the sex workers drew on their own experience to interpret the text. For instance, the moment where Tamar takes off her widow's garments and puts on the veil to get herself ready to sit at the city gate and encounter Judah, reminded them of their own difficulties and fears in determining to become sex workers. It also reminded them of the lengths they go to to preserve their privacy and hide their profession from family. Another example is how the sex workers identified the threat of verbal abuse and sexual harassment in public places of Hong Kong where men dominate, and they applied this to imagining Tamar at the gate at the time when men were gathering for the sheep shearing. Once more, this makes us appreciate more acutely how vulnerable and how brave Tamar is. To give a final example, the sex workers recognised that in both Genesis 38 and in their own setting, men who seek sexual gratification are excused, while women and especially prostitutes are chastised for having sex or wanting sex. Sometimes this takes the form of exclusion. They have encountered this with some Christians who consider "being a Christian" and "being a sex worker" mutually exclusive.

Let me turn for more insights to another biblical text.

Notes

1 Andrew Chiu, *The Book of Genesis* (Chinese Bible Commentary Vol. 2, Hong Kong: Chinese Christian Literature, 1992), 501–7.
2 Andrew P.C. Kwong, *Genesis*, Vol. 4 Tien Dao Bible Commentary (Hong Kong: Tien Dao, 2015). Kwong frequently cites Gordon J. Wenham, *Genesis 16–50* (Word Biblical Commentary, 2; Waco, TX: Word, 1994); John H. Sailmaiher, *Genesis* (The Expositor's Bible Commentary; rev. ed.; Grand Rapids, MI: Zondervan, 2008) and Victor P. Hamilton, *The Book of Genesis 18–50* (New International Commentary of the Old Testament; Grand Rapids, MI: Wm B. Eerdmans, 1995).
3 As there is no attribution of an author's name for these two excerpts, I shall use the abbreviation DDW2 for volume 2 and DDW3 for volume 3, respectively.
4 Chiu, 502–3. The Chinese language also has the word 克 *kefu* where 妇 *fu* refers to the wife—here the husband is the cause of the wife's suffering and death.
5 Kwong, 369.
6 DDW2, 55.
7 DDW3, 67.
8 Chiu, 504.
9 Chiu, 504.
10 Kwong, 373–74; Kwong interprets the narratives in Genesis intertextually. Thus, he draws analogies between this story and that of David's encounter with Bathsheba: in both stories male protagonists "see" and act on their lust. Cf. 390–2.
11 Kwong, 376.

12 Chiu, 504.
13 Kwong, 372 n. 79.
14 Chiu, 505.
15 Kwong, 378–9. He cites B.Vawter, *Amos, Hosea, Micah* (Wilmington, NC: Michael Glazier, 1981), p. 94.
16 Chiu, 506; and Kwong, 371 see his n. 69.
17 Chiu, 506.
18 Kwong, 381.
19 Chiu, 506.
20 Chiu, 506–7.
21 Chiu, 507.
22 Kwong, 382.
23 Kwong, 385, 387. He repeats this adjective in the later section titled "Application", 396.
24 According to the sex workers, they do not offer the complete range of sexual services. They only list those they feel comfortable to provide.
25 Janzen, *Gen 12–50: Abraham and All the Families of the Earth* (International Theological Commentary; Grand Rapids, MI: Eerdmans, 1993), 154.
26 Kwong, 372.
27 Chiu, 501; John E. Hartley, following Claus Westermann, compares the themes of losing a son and wife in Genesis 37 and 38. See Hartley, *Genesis* (New International Biblical Commentary, vol. 1; Carlisle, Cumbria: Paternoster, 2000), 316; and Westermann, *Genesis 37–50* (Continental Commentary Series; trans. John J. Scullion S.J.; London: Society for Promoting Christian Knowledge/Minneapolis, MN: Augsburg, 1986), 52. The only one that seems to show more empathy for Tamar is Terrence Fretheim, who mentions Judah does this "at the expense" of Tamar. Fretheim, *Genesis* (New Interpreter's Bible; New York: Abingdon), 605.
28 Genesis 19 recounts the incident when the angels of YHWH visit Abraham's nephew Lot in Sodom to warn him and to escort his family out of the city before YHWH sends his destruction. The people of Sodom see the strangers entering Lot's residence and pound on his door, demanding Lot surrender them so that they may "know" them (commonly used as a euphemism for sexual intercourse or, in this case, rape). Lot's initial reply to the men of the city is that he is going to offer his two daughters who have not "known" any men, and they may do to them whatever they wish (v.8). Fortunately, before any violence befalls Lot's two daughters, the angels save the whole family by striking blind the men outside Lot's door. The family flees Sodom while the destruction of the city takes place. In the next story found in Judges 19–21, the women are not as fortunate. The first victim to be offered up is a concubine of a Levite man. She had left her husband for her father's house but her husband seeks for her return. Her father delays their departure and on their journey home, the couple are found without accommodation for the night in the town of Gibeah, belonging to the tribe of Benjamin. An old man from Ephraim but resident at Gibeah takes them in and provides hospitality for the couple. However, in the night, some ruthless men from the city demand that the old man surrender the Levite because they want to "know" him. The old man goes out to plead with the men by offering his own virgin daughter and the man's concubine in the Levite's stead (19:24). But as the old man returns to his door, the Levite grabs his concubine and throws her out of the house for the reckless men, then shutting the door. The men rape the concubine until morning, and she falls down motionless at the

door of the house. The Levite wakes up and prepares for the journey. Seeing his concubine lying on the ground at the door, he tells her to get up, but there is no response. He takes her body and places her on the donkey and heads home. When he returns to his house, he slaughters the concubine, cutting her into twelve parts and sends these with his men to all the towns of Israel, demanding justice for what has happened to him. The people of Israel gather before the man who complains to them that when he was passing by Gibeah the leaders there wanted to kill him and they raped his concubine until she died. So the people of Israel decide they would go to Gibeah, bring out those men responsible for the deed, and punish them. The Benjaminites, however, refuse to surrender the men responsible. Having sought guidance from YHWH, Israel goes to war with the tribe of Benjamin for three days, and each day begins with them seeking YHWH and obeying his instructions. On the final day, Israel burns and kills all the people, livestock and everything that once belonged to the towns of the tribe, except for 600 men who escape and hide in the rocks of Rimmon. Four months later, all the tribes of Israel gather together. They promise not to give their daughters to the 600 Benjaminites. However, they then begin to mourn for the loss of this tribe before their God, and it seems they do not wish that the tribe should be wiped out. After offering their sacrifices to God, the men of Israel discover that the people of Jabesh-gilead had abstained from attending the gathering and sacrifice at Mizpah, which apparently, all Israel had to attend. As punishment for their absence, they send 12,000 men to kill the men and all the women who had given birth and had had sexual intercourse with men. The remaining female virgins were allowed to live and, when counted, were 400 in number. The men brought them to the camp at Shiloh, and the leaders of Israel agreed to give these 400 women to the Benjaminites and to allow them to return to their towns to rebuild them. However, 400 women were insufficient for the 600 men. To resolve this problem, the men of Israel told the Benjaminites who had not acquired wives that they should hide in ambush during a festival at Shiloh and when their women come out to celebrate, the Benjaminites should seize any woman they wished. The men of Israel guaranteed the Benjaminites that they would vouch for their actions should the fathers and brothers of these women from Shiloh complain. This bizarre account of at least three incidents of gang rape and of wars, sanctioned by YHWH, is one of the most distressing stories in the Hebrew Bible. Both the stories in Genesis 19 and Judges 19–21 depict women as dispensable commodities to serve men's and their God's purposes.

29 Sarah Shectman, *Women in the Pentateuch: A Feminist and Source-Critical Analysis* (Hebrew Bible Monographs, 23; Sheffield: Sheffield Phoenix, 2009), 106; Fretheim, 605.

30 Michael Astour, "Tamar the Hierodule: An Essay in the Method of Vestigial Motifs", *Journal of Biblical Literature* 85 (1966): 185–96; Joan G. Westernholz, "Tamar, Qĕdēšā, Qadištu, and Sacred Prostitution in Mesopotamia", *Harvard Theological Review* 82.3 (1989): 245–65; Fretheim, 605; Westermann, 53.

31 Tammi J. Schneider, *Mothers of Promise: Women in the Book of Genesis* (Ada, MI: Baker Academic, 2008), 153–4. Schneider employs this interpretation to argue that Tamar waits at the gate for Judah in order to confront him, rather than seduce him. However, when he sees her, he solicits her services and she then decides to go along with his proposal. None of the sex workers considered this possibility. If indeed this is Tamar's intention, then there is no need for Tamar to change from her widow's garments and veil herself.

32 Wenham, 366. In Biblical Hebrew, the waw-consecutive or *wayyiqtol* verb has the function of showing the "succession" of actions in a narrative. Also sometimes known as the "narrative verb", the consecutive occurrences of these verbs indicate the main storyline in a narrative. Cf. Paul Joüon and Takamitsu Muraoka, *A Grammar of Biblical Hebrew* (Subsidia Biblical, 27; Roma: Pontificio Intituto Biblico, 2006), 360–7.
33 Jione Havea, *Elusions of Control: Biblical Law on the Words of Women* (Leiden/Boston, MA: Brill, 2003), 165–76.
34 Westermann, 53; Derek Kidner, *Genesis: An Introduction and Commentary* (Tyndale Old Testament Commentary; Leicester, England/Downer's Grove, IL: Intervarsity Press, 1967), 188; Hartley, 318.
35 Hamilton, 447; Bird, "The Harlot as Heroine: Narrative and Social Presupposition in Three Old Testament Texts", in *Missing Persons and Mistaken Identities: Women and Gender in Ancient Israel* (Minneapolis, MN: Fortress Press, 1997), 216.
36 Chiu, 505. He also cites an earlier Chinese scholar's commentary: Y.Z. Tang, *Commentary on Genesis* (Hong Kong: Tien Dao, 1972). DDW3 also presents Tamar as a temple prostitute.
37 Kwong, 385–7.

4 Sex workers read the story of the two prostitutes and King Solomon

Mei-Ling is from Mainland China and her husband is working in Hong Kong. She wants to provide more financial support for her elderly parents and, after trying jobs at a restaurant and as a masseuse, decides to turn to sex work. She told Amnesty International her story about her first week as a sex worker:

> ... an undercover *male police* officer approached her on the street and asked to buy sex from her. They went to her flat, where he arrested her. Several officers searched the flat after her arrest and seized condoms and [used] tissues to use as evidence.
>
> The police took Mei-Ling to the Tai Po station. "I was not informed of my rights," she told Amnesty International. "My mobile was taken away from me. I was kept there for 15 hours—there were two officers non-stop asking me questions. One officer was nice; the other was very mean.
>
> They showed me a statement. Some parts of it were true, but others were untrue. The statement said that I approached the police—but it was the police who approached me. They said I was soliciting the police, but I was soliciting another person (before the undercover *police officer* approached her). The officers asked me to sign (the statement) but I didn't want to sign it."
>
> The officers threatened to call her husband, a civil servant, and her daughter if she did not sign the statement. "I didn't want them to find out," she said. "The nice officer told me I could change the statement later—he said he would help me do an appeal. He said that if I deny the charge, I can just defend myself later in court. He told me that because I'm not a Hong Kong resident, it would not be a problem for me, because one-to-one service is not illegal."
> Mei-Ling was told she could not call her teenage daughter to tell her

where she was until the statement had been signed and *she* was not given a copy of her statement.

She was charged with solicitation, and she denied the charge when she appeared in court. "I thought the court would be fair—I had confidence in the court—but not any more. I was very disappointed because the police swore (an oath to tell) the truth—but (what they said) wasn't the truth."

Beginning to cry, she continued: "I was very angry because at that time, my husband was not giving me enough money for living—mother and father were very ill and I needed money for medicine. But the judge said 'you're not acting responsibly towards your family—you're supposed to know the result of doing this kind of work.'"

She told Amnesty International that she felt powerless to challenge the police account of the events that led to her arrest. "I couldn't make any complaint because there were no witnesses—and the statement was so perfect. In the court, my lawyer asked the police to describe what I was wearing and they couldn't. But even after such a big mistake, the court believed the police, so making a complaint would be useless."

Mei-Ling was found guilty of solicitation and sentenced to four months in prison. "I'm still very angry with the police," she said. "The court also made me very angry—the court judged me not responsible towards my family, and I was given the most serious punishment."[1]

Mei-Ling, trapped by the undercover officer, betrayed by the legal system that distorted her testimony, felt humiliated in court and belittled for her filial piety. She received an excessive punishment for a victimless "crime". The court rarely takes a sex worker's testimony seriously but especially when it is against a police statement. Such corruption only encourages more police abuse and more violence against sex workers. There are many similar stories where the court and legal system cause miscarriages of justice for sex workers—and one also finds a similar story in the Hebrew Bible, namely, the tale of the two prostitutes and Solomon in 1 Kings 3:16–28.

Rape myths propagate the untruth that when women are "properly" assaulted, they will scream, kick and do everything they can to fight and escape. Those who do not retaliate physically are not "really" raped. This myth is propagated at every court case where the attorney for the person accused of rape questions and challenges victims for not fighting back but claiming they were raped.[2] According to a forensic psychologist, however, the reaction of fighting back and attempting to escape happens, but it is rarely the usual response.[3] This myth seems to be reflected in Deuteronomy 22:23–7, where an engaged woman is pardoned from the death sentence for adultery if she is raped in an open field, because she may have cried out, yet no one could hear her.[4] If, however, a woman is raped in a town and does not cry out and is discovered, then she is sentenced to death along with her assailant—because she could not have resisted "properly" and should have cried loudly and alerted others to her plight. This myth oversimplifies the situation of rape and ignores that many victims report "freezing". Moreover, when a rapist is not a stranger but known to the victim, there can be additional complexities. And herein lies another popular rape myth: namely, that "real" rapes are committed by strangers. Instead, the opposite is true: far more rapes are committed by persons known to their victims (see Chapter 2, endnote 19).

This chapter will report on the reading of the story of the two prostitutes and King Solomon with the sex workers.[5] This story is not a rape text per se, but the sex workers' standpoint to the story explains why rapes are so often not reported, especially when the victims are sex workers. Their stories inform the deep stigmatization of sex workers by the police and courts of justice and their insights carry over into the interpretation of this story.

4.1 The story of the two prostitutes and King Solomon

Prior to the story in 1 Kings 3:16–22, vv.3–15 narrate how the newly ordained King Solomon asked YHWH for wisdom. Delighted by his noble request, YHWH promised to grant Solomon riches and fame as well as wisdom, on the condition that he should keep the terms of the divine covenant like his father David had. After this follows the (in)famous story of the two prostitutes.

Two prostitutes come before the king with their stories. They have been living together and had given birth to sons three days apart. The first complainant explains that the other woman had lain on her own son and he had subsequently died; the mother had then exchanged her dead son for the live one of the other woman. So, when the first complainant awoke, she discovered the dead child but soon realised it was not hers. Both women claimed that the living son was theirs and they argued their case before the king. The king asked for a sword to be brought out and declared that the infant was to be cut into two, with each woman to receive one half. At that instant, the mother of the living infant begged the king to let the child live, while the other woman declared that the king's will be done so that neither should have a son. The king announced that the living son was to be handed to the woman who had attempted to stop the slaughter of the infant, recognising her to be the mother. The story ends with "all Israel … stood in fear of the king".

4.2 Hong Kong Christian interpretations

There are two popular Chinese commentaries: the first, on 1 and 2 Kings, is by Tsai Rei Yi, whose work is published by the Chinese Bible Commentary series in one volume;[6] the second is by Paul Li, whose commentary comes in two volumes with the Tien Dao Bible Commentary series.[7] DDW2 and DDW3 do not have any comment on this passage. Discussion on how these two commentators identify the purpose of the narrative and how they portray and interpret the two prostitutes now follows.

4.2.1 Purpose of the story

These two commentaries, like most Western exegeses, affirm that the purpose of this narrative is to exalt Solomon's wisdom and confirm it as divinely ordained. No one could resolve this difficult situation so effectively except with God's help. Solomon's wisdom is evidence of God's election of him as Israel's ruler. Nonetheless, the two commentators interpret differently how the case came about and also the implications of this event.

Tsai proposes that this incident is testimony to even prostitutes, being the basest of all the population of Israel, receiving King Solomon's attention, wise counsel and justice. For Tsai, this narrative exemplifies the king's care and magnanimity for *all* his people. Thus, Israel rightly reveres Solomon.[8]

In contrast to this view, Li argues that commoners' cases were resolved at the district court without needing the king's personal attention. He posits that the local judges could not resolve the case and that is why it was brought to Solomon.[9] Li also puts forward the proposition that the verb in 3:16 ("two prostitutes *came* to the king") could also have passive force: so one might read, "the prostitutes *were brought* before the king". But a direct object is lacking and the verb appears to be a regular active form, hence there is no leeway for this suggestion. Li's view is that the prostitutes did not seek out the king to resolve their case, i.e. because Solomon was close to the people or because he was known to be kind. Li adds that despite the fact that the mothers were prostitutes, they, nonetheless, deserve justice. Hence Li and Tsai's commentaries diverge a little.

4.2.2 Interpretations concerning the prostitutes

Tsai describes prostitutes depicted in the Bible as the lowest-ranking people of society who are least likely to receive a hearing, let alone justice.[10] In her conclusion, she pits the true mother's love against the selfish desires of the other woman. Without mentioning that the mothers are prostitutes, she presents the story as one demonstrating the nature of maternal love: love relinquishes and puts the beloved before oneself. She goes on to say that false love seeks only to possess and to insist on making claims to ownership, regardless of the harm and hurt caused to another and without capacity for remorse. Tsai refuses, however, to identify the biological mother. Her point is that the one who truly loves the child deserves to nurture the infant, irrespective of biology.

Li takes six pages in total to argue who the real mother is.[11] In summary, he concludes that the one who first talks and is able to describe the situation vividly cannot be the real mother. Li calls the false mother "evil".[12] He deduces that the problem in this case is that there are no witnesses. He also imagines that these two women might have been best friends earlier and decided to help each other out. He believes Solomon already knows the answer but there is no evidence, so he resorts to working with the emotions of the women. The sword is only an instrument in the pretence of being fair.[13] For Li, the fact that the story concludes without informing readers of what happens to the mother who lied indicates that the outcome is not the ultimate purpose of the narrative. Rather, the verses following, describing how all Israel feared Solomon, gets to the true purpose. The point of the story is not to find justice for the mother but for Israelites to recognise that God has chosen a very wise king to rule over them.[14]

4.3 Sex workers' standpoints

We have seen that the Chinese commentators accept the negative assessment that prostitutes are base, belong to the lowest stratum of society, and do not often receive justice under the law. The two commentators remark that these two prostitutes are privileged to be able to come before their king. In addition, they are also quick to judge the mother whose infant died: Tsai calls her actions "false love" and Li refers to her as "evil". The sex workers' standpoints cast a different light on the prostitutes in the story.

4.3.1 Sympathy for the two prostitutes

After we read the story, the sex workers expressed sympathy for the two prostitutes. They felt empathy for anyone who desires to be a mother, especially in difficult circumstances. The sex workers believed that the mother whose child died must be suffering from acute grief and could not accept the death of her baby son. So, either she must have made up the story or done the things to the other mother but without being in her right mind. She acts out of a surge of overwhelming emotions. The sex workers felt that she should not be condemned and judged because she clearly needs help. They actually appreciated the fact that at the end of the story the king does not pronounce a sentence on the mother who agreed with him to cut the infant into two.

When compared with the sex workers' response, hardly any commentators, Chinese or Western, give much thought to the emotional states of the two prostitutes. Avaren Ipsen's reading group expressed sympathy for the prostitutes but did not go as far as to mention the emotional stability of post-natal mothers.[15] This is an important point to mention here as it provides further evidence (as if it should be needed) to show that sex workers are not thoughtless, heartless, opportunist, unethical or immoral human beings, or bad mothers—which are prejudices with which they are often confronted.

Ipsen presents an important observation in her readings: sex workers sympathise with the two prostitutes because they are also, in very many cases, mothers.[16] As mentioned in Chapters 1 and 2, today's sex workers were very often mothers first before they took on the profession. In our world, economic inequality, discrimination against women in the workplace and the gender pay gap are factors that drive mothers, especially mothers restricted through financial need and the need for flexible working hours, into sex work.[17] Perhaps this biblical story portrays a reverse of the situation; perhaps these two women were prostitutes first[18] and then mothers. The sex workers, however, maintained their esteem for the two mothers in the narrative. Indeed, they expressed a strong sense of connection to the plight of *both* women in the story. This connection extends also to the two infants in the story: the dead one is grieved for and the living one is wished love, respect and care. Nevertheless, overall, the sex workers find this story highly problematic in a number of ways.

4.3.2 Violence disguised as wisdom

At the start of the discussion, after we had read the story, the sex workers made comments similar to those of Tsai: that Solomon must be a good king because the prostitutes show no fear approaching him. This openness and accessibility are contrary to the experiences of Hong Kong sex workers today, given that police stations and courts are not experienced as places where they feel heard or are shown respect. The sex workers shared their bitter experience that whenever personnel at the police or court realise they are sex workers, attitudes change from neutral to disrespectful. Whatever they had to say was suddenly not taken seriously, and the police treated them as if they had no right to be at either the police station or court, or to make any complaint against anyone. Ipsen's group shared similar experiences with law and order. The main difference, however, is that sex work in the San Francisco Bay area is criminalised and so, to go to the police station with a complaint was all the more risky and could transpire in a sex worker getting imprisoned or fined. Both groups of sex workers reported finding themselves on the wrong side of the law and both reported that their complaints and cases were most often not handled justly. This Bible story about the two prostitutes approaching the king to seek justice does not in any way match the reality of their experiences. The sex workers in my group actually wondered if there was a time in the past when sex workers were more respected, even by the king. Otherwise, they concluded, this king must be a particularly kind example if the prostitutes can trust him to enact justice on their behalf.

As the discussion progressed, however, the sex workers' view of Solomon gradually changed. They started to question his intelligence and his wisdom. To them, witnesses need not just be people who had been with the prostitutes at the time when one of the infants died. Witnesses should also have included people who had acquaintance with them: such as midwives, the bread seller from whom they regularly purchased bread, or the other prostitutes who knew them. Such witnesses could have provided character references. Furthermore, evidence at the scene of the crime could have been collected. They considered that since tests for DNA were not available back then, there might have been other clues, such as any marks, etc. on the body of the dead infant, or on the cloths used to wrap the infants. The sex workers felt that there was an insufficient attempt to investigate the matter more fully before the sword was called into play.

This sword, for the sex workers, symbolises violence. Violence is frightening for the sex workers and they experience it often, not only in the context of their work but also from police officers, at police stations and in courts. It is the tool used against them to silence them and to stop questions about their rights, to intimidate them and to deprive them of justice. In this story, they decide, neither prostitute wins and the surviving child, too, might be negatively impacted. The women's and the child's reputation and future prospects are made vulnerable through the exposure of both the women's profession and of their case before the king himself. Moreover, the judgement is overshadowed by violence and fear, given the presence of the sword. No one trusted either of their testimonies, signifying suspicion and disdain of prostitutes. By implication, only the sword, the threat of killing, can evoke the truth from persons like them. The sex workers also raised this question: what if the prostitutes had not responded in the way Solomon expected them to respond? The sex workers felt it was more likely that neither prostitute would allow Solomon to cut the baby in half, not just the "real" mother. They considered Solomon's alleged intelligence to be highly problematic. He had no understanding of women's emotions and especially not those of post-natal women. The sex workers also observed that Solomon did not demonstrate compassion or speak kindly to the two prostitutes. They opined that when Solomon ordered the sword, everyone in the courtroom must have been terrified, including the other prostitute who had agreed with the king's judgement. What she uttered, if she really did utter the words recorded (3:26b), might not have been in a heartless and selfish tone, but in a horrified one, upon recognising that the king was much more cruel than expected. What a king commands is obeyed and not defied. The lives of the prostitutes were at stake as well, not just the living infant's life. Hence, to go along with the king's wishes may have been what was in the mind of the woman: she wants to survive.

Fear of a superior's order is something that the sex workers said they were familiar with. They often complied with orders that terrified them and suffered the consequences silently. The sex workers were all too familiar with coercion by police or by people who pretended to be police. Police officers often found reasons to arrest them or threaten to report them to their families and children, and in exchange for letting them off, the sex workers would have to provide them with free sexual services. At times the police not only left without paying but also took their earnings as well.

The sex workers used a local language term for this: 霸王食 *bawang can*, which literally means "an overlord's meal". What it refers to is rape: coerced free-of-charge sex. Zi Teng reported an incident to Amnesty International[19] where a police officer showed up at a sex worker's apartment and announced that he was there to check her documents. She dutifully produced her documents. He then drew out his gun, and with a HK$20 note (US$2.50), placed the note under the gun on the table and asked if she would provide sexual services. The rate for these sexual services, however, was in the range of HK$300–500 (US$38.00–$65.00) at that time. The sex worker understood the gun to be a threat to arrest her, or harm her. Under such circumstances, when a police officer is the perpetrator, to whom could the sex worker report? Could she really retaliate, such as by kicking, yelling or running away? And in the absence of such actions, could she really make a case for non-consent and rape? The sex workers, telling similar stories, described very evocatively their lack of recourse to justice.

Not only sex workers themselves, but a lawyer, too, told Amnesty International that police often target sex workers, particularly those from Mainland China.[20] But even if sex workers have compelling complaints against police and legal representation, they often choose to abort the legal process and instead agree to be sent home. This is because, as in Mei-Ling's story at the beginning of this chapter, there is legitimate concern that police will distort sex workers' accounts and obstruct their access to a fair or full hearing.

Ms Sherry Hui of JJJ told me in our interview[21] that all the sisters are afraid of being raped and that rape, whether by clients or police, occurs regularly. The sex workers usually choose not to report rape, because encountering police for this purpose is another ordeal in itself. Even if it is not rape that is committed against them, but instead theft or burglary, or being scammed, sex workers often prefer to avoid *any* encounter with police. The reason is simple—the police do not respect them as citizens with full rights to justice, but will often intimidate or belittle them and often do not take their testimonies seriously. Worse still, some officers, both male and female, find reasons to arrest them. Similarly, the courts are not always impartial when it comes to sex workers, instead judging them. This is borne out by a case where a judge sentenced a police officer to twenty months' imprisonment for having abused his authority when he did not pay a sex worker for her services and threatened her with arrest.[22] At first view this might seem laudable. But first, the police officer was not charged with rape in this case and second, the judge also told the sex worker that she should be tried for breaching immigration laws, thereby downplaying that she was the victim of a crime.

The sex workers' ongoing plight, being at risk of and suffering rape, without even having this acknowledged as rape, is a grave injustice and shows that rape myths have triumphed. Sex workers are compelled to accept what the police and the courts of law make of and have decided about them. With regard to the biblical story, the prostitutes' voices are subsumed by praise for Solomon. Like the Hong Kong sex workers, in the face of authority they are silenced. Perhaps the prostitute who agrees with the king about cutting the baby in two is only trying to protect herself. Succumbing to and accepting violence is certainly something that resonated with the sex workers.

Solomon's sword and his command indicate he is a violent judge. Ultimately, therefore, it is difficult for the sex workers to trust him. The sex workers sighed helplessly, because this scenario, with the presence of threat and coercion, is not entirely dissimilar from their experiences of dealings with police and courts. Matters regarding prostitutes' lives were not better in earlier times as they had thought initially. They began to mistrust the cleverness and the guise of benevolence in this story.

Li seems to fill the gap identified by the sex workers (about fuller investigation being wanting) by suggesting that local courts had actually conducted such work but that they failed to resolve matters and then brought the difficult case before the wise king.[23] Li's proposition enhances Solomon's reputation yet more: only *he* can succeed where all others before him failed. Like the sex workers in both my group and Ipsen's, however, the rabbis of the medieval period, too, faulted Solomon on two counts: the lack of witnesses, and bringing out the sword too soon.[24] Both Tsai and Li fail to acknowledge that the sword is an aggressive, even brutal, sign, instead praising Solomon profusely for his divinely endowed wisdom. Contrastingly, both Walter Brueggemann and Choon-Leong Seow point out that the sword is a violent expression of justice and wisdom.[25] The reaction to Solomon's action is thus mixed.

Seow also raises other questions similar to those of the sex workers, namely whether investigation by the royal judiciary was inadequate.[26] Seow also expresses doubts about interpreting at face value the way the two mothers respond following Solomon's order to split the baby in half. Again, like the sex workers proposed, it is worthy of consideration that fear for her life may have made the other prostitute accept the king's order.

4.3.3 *The biblical author marginalises the prostitutes and their children*

Next, the sex workers began to question why these two women were introduced as prostitutes (3:16), and what the purpose of this was in the story. The modern-day sex workers did not think that the practice of two women living together would impute they were prostitutes (3:17). The two women could merely be good friends, or they might be a support for each other, with both being single mothers—perhaps one or both had left their husband. (It is my judgement, too, that women in antiquity could have lived together for other reasons, such as in menstruation huts during times of impurity, including after giving birth.[27] In such cases even "respectable" women would live together.) The sex workers deduced two possibilities to account for identifying the women as prostitutes: first, "sex sells" and second, the biblical author is biased against prostitutes.

Regarding the notion that "sex sells", the sex workers argued for this being the author's way of making his (the sex workers believed the author to be male) piece more popular to an audience. By making two characters in this story prostitutes, a reader or listener, maybe expecting sexual content, might be more eager to listen up, or read on. Alternatively, they concluded, the author has an aversion to prostitutes. For evidence of this, they point out that he has portrayed the prostitutes as deceptive, or, at least, as unreliable witnesses. Moreover, their presence draws a sharp contrast between Solomon the king, of the highest rank in the society, and the prostitutes, among the lowest and basest of society. While it may appear as though Solomon discharged justice *even* for prostitutes, in actual fact, this is yet another story that threatens sex workers by affirming their marginal and lowly status. The sex workers expressed indignation that the sword is directed against the helpless infant belonging to one of the prostitutes. The sex workers considered this portrayal in the Bible to be severely threatening to them and their children. Moreover, they argued that Solomon is exalted at their expense.

No commentator takes the biblical author to task with the vigour shown by the sex workers. Nonetheless, some scholars *do* raise the question as to why this story portrays the two unnamed women as prostitutes.[28] Scholarship brings to light the fact that this story plot is a common one in ancient cultures, and while elsewhere, the female characters are not identified as prostitutes, the male character is often the ruler.[29] Hence, it is a formulaic device for the author to highlight the wisdom of the king, Solomon in this case. As for the mention of "prostitutes" instead of just "mothers", the most commonly argued theory is that the story requires the two women to be staying together at the time of the birth of the infants—and so, for the biblical author, these women who have children and who live independently of men cannot be respectable wives, or respectable unmarried sisters, but must be "prostitutes".[30] Noteworthy here is the fact that the Hebrew narrative mentions the word "prostitutes" only in v.16, while the remainder of the narrative refers to "women".

Mordechai Cogan suggests that the author wants to present Solomon as the king who superseded David. After all, David had been faulted for not listening to the people's cause (2 Samuel 15:3).[31] So here, two persons from the lowest stratum of society, "women" and, moreover, "prostitutes", receive attention from the king. This explanation is largely accepted and is repeated in both Tsai and Li's works.

From another angle, Ipsen points out that much of the cause of, and rise in, prostitution originates in political and economic factors— more especially, in severe economic disparity where women's work and contributions in the domestic sphere are low in value.³² Therefore, to talk about sex work without reference to political and economic factors is not helpful. With regard to this biblical narrative, Ipsen accepts David Jobling's proposition on the problematic portrayal of Solomon's "golden era" from 1 Kings 3–11. Consequently, the appearance of prostitutes signals actual political and economic fractures that are obscured by this claim.³³

As I have discussed elsewhere, it is important to register other female presences in narratives of Solomon: not only the appearance of the two prostitutes in this passage, but also, just earlier, of Pharaoh's daughter (1 Kings 3:1) and especially the mention of Solomon's many other foreign wives, particularly with reference to his downfall (1 Kings 11:1–11). All of these mentions of women might actually hint that the author's confidence in Solomon's kingship and wisdom is not as steadfast as most commentators of 1 Kings 3:16–28 have taken it to be.³⁴

In a similar vein, and also suggesting hints of criticism of Solomon, Ipsen proposes that המלך מפני ויראו in v.28, often translated as "they stood in awe of the king", or similar, and taken to signify that Israel was awestruck on account of the king's wisdom, could also be rendered, "they were scared off from the presence of the king".³⁵ Of course, the Hong Kong sex workers have neither read all of 1 Kings 1–11, nor do they read Hebrew, but their interpretations expressing suspicion and fear of Solomon, compel us to re-examine conventional interpretations.

The sex workers in Ipsen's group also resisted the way the story creates enmity between the prostitutes: one good and the other bad; one tender and maternal and one cruel and willing to see a baby killed; one deserving and the other unworthy.³⁶ Ipsen also cites Claudia Camp who criticises this narrative for making the two prostitutes adversaries, so that when the sword is brought out, one or other must lose.³⁷ These literary tools employed by the author are not well received by the sex workers and only amplify their perception of how prejudiced the author is against prostitutes. As they point out, whether this is deliberate or inadvertent, the story promotes marginalization of sex workers right up to today.

4.4 Chapter summary

The sex workers' standpoints differ drastically from those of the Chinese commentators and from those of most Western scholarship. The commentators tend to interpret the story as a confirmation of Solomon's extraordinary wisdom, wisdom that could only come from God. The sex workers interpret the story otherwise, as a story of violence and threat and of prejudice against prostitutes.

The sex workers' standpoints lead us to re-read the story in a different light. The sex workers' perspectives and testimonies show how the police and law courts often find ways to entrap them, to twist their testimonies, to subvert their full rights, and to criminalise their actions. Thus, the sex workers are more often on the "wrong" side of the law. Bringing such experiences to the biblical text, the story, according to the sex workers, aids stigmatization of sex workers. As I have illustrated, the same charge can be levelled, too, at the conventional interpretations of this story.

For the sex workers, the story is demeaning to prostitutes, portraying them as unreliable witnesses in court, and as deserving of violence, or as responding only to threats of violence. A veneer of "divinely granted wisdom" shrouds terrible violence. Deadly violence is threatened and even though the infant's life is spared, any solidarity between the two prostitutes is destroyed. How will their lives look going forward? Will either still have a home to go to after this? Without the income of the other, can either live in the place they once shared? Can the women or the child survive this impending threat of poverty?

The sex workers' interpretation also shows how deep-seated stigmatization of sex workers can promote rape myths such as the myth that "sex workers cannot be raped". The myth encourages abusive behaviour against sex workers by police officers and clients alike. However, the sex workers' standpoints also help to debunk this myth, alongside another rape myth that a victim of rape must put up strong physical resistance and show evidence of such resistance to prove rape has occurred. The sex workers' accounts of abuse and threats from police officers and clients inform us that rape victims are often coerced to comply with their perpetrators. Furthermore, there is no "formula" for responding to rape: some rape victims fight, others become terrified into passivity. There is too little compassion and support—both for the prostitutes of the story and for the sex workers of Hong Kong and elsewhere. The insights brought to this story in 1 Kings through the sex workers' standpoints, have, however, shed new light on and brought more urgency to the matter of justice for sex workers and rape victims.

Notes

1 This story is quoted directly from the published study by Amnesty International, *Harmfully Isolated* (London: Amnesty International, 2016), 8. The italics are mine and added to clarify the sentences.
2 The most recent publicised case was reported by Melissa Chan, "In Harvey Weinstein Trial, Drama Gives Way to Lesson on 'Rape Myths'", *Time*, 24 January 2020. https://time.com/5771482/harvey-weinstein-trial-rape-sciorra-2/.

3   Ibid.
4   Susanne Scholz, *Sacred Witness: Rape in the Hebrew Bible* (Minneapolis, MN: Fortress, 2014), 115–17.
5   As mentioned earlier, part of the sex workers' interpretations and the engagement with scholarship mentioned in this chapter were published in 2014, cf. Tan, 157–78.
6   Tsai Rei Yi, *I & II Kings* (Chinese Bible Commentary, vol. 10; Hong Kong: Chinese Christian Council, 2002).
7   Paul Li, *I Kings* (Tien Dao Bible Commentary; Hong Kong: Tien Dao, 2003).
8   Tsai, 122.
9   Li, 305.
10 Tsai, 122.
11 Li, 307–13.
12 Li, 309.
13 Li, 312–13.
14 Li, 313.
15 Cf., Avaren Ipsen, *Sex Working and the Bible* (London: Equinox, 2009), 108.
16 Ipsen, 99.
17 Ipsen, 94–7.
18 The story does not mention if the two infants were the mothers' first-born children.
19 *Harmfully Isolated*, 21.
20 Ibid.
21 Cf. Chapter 1, note 3. The sex workers often mentioned *bawong can* ("the overlord's meal") casually during the reading exercises, but they did not go into any detail. They admitted they had complied with police demands but said little more.
22 *Harmfully Isolated*, 21–2.
23 Li, 305.
24 Angel Hayyim, "Cut the Baby in Half: Understanding Solomon's Divine Wisdom," *JBQ* 39.3 (2011): 189–94.
25 Walter Brueggemann, *1 & 2 Kings* (Smith and Helwys Bible Commentary; Macon, GA: Smith and Helwys, 2000), 54–5; and Choon-Leong Seow, *1 & 2 Kings* (The New Interpreter's Bible, vol. 3; Nashville, TN: Abingdon, 1999), 45–6. Seow, a Chinese biblical scholar, offers an extraordinary and inclusive interpretation on the books of Kings but this commentary is not available in Chinese yet.
26 Seow, 44.
27 Ibid.
28 Hugh Pyper, "Judging the Wisdom of Solomon: The Two-Way Effect of Intertextuality", *Journal for the Study of the Old Testament* 59 (1993): 25–36. Ipsen takes this question and explores it further in the light of political and economic factors (Ipsen, 92–113).
29 James A. Montgomery, *A Critical and Exegetical Commentary on the Book of Kings* (International Critical Commentary; Edinburgh: T & T Clark, 1951), 109; Gwilym H. Jones, *1 and 2 Kings* (New Century Bible Commentary, vol. 1; Grand Rapids, MI: W. B. Eerdmans/London: Marshall, Morgan & Scott, 1984), 130–1. Ipsen mentions that in folklore "widows" is more common, citing H. Gressman, "Das Solomonische Urteil", *Deutsche Rundschau* 130 (1907): 212–8; and Theodor Gaster, *Myth, Legend, and Custom in the Old Testament* (Gloucester: Peter Smith, 1981, II), 491–4.

30 Mordechai Cogan, *1 Kings: A New Translation with Introduction and Commentary* (Anchor Bible, 10; New York: Doubleday, 2001), 193.
31 Ibid.
32 Ipsen, 92–6.
33 Ipsen, 95, 107. Cf. Jobling, "'Forced Labour': Solomon's Golden Age and the Question of Literary Representation", *Semeia* 54 (1992): 57–76.
34 Tan, 172–5.
35 Ipsen, 98.
36 Ipsen, 98–9.
37 Ipsen, 105. Cf. C.V. Camp, "1 and 2 Kings", in *The Women's Bible Commentary*, eds. C.A. Newsom and Sharon Ringe (Louisville, KY: Westminster/John Knox, 1992), 100.

5 Sex workers read Gomer and the female prostitution figures in Hosea 1–3

The discussion in the last two chapters has shown how the sex workers' standpoint readings of Genesis 38 and 1 Kings 3:16–28 are redolent with their experiences of various forms of injustice, including mistreatment at the hands of the Hong Kong police, law courts, clients and the public. In this chapter, the discussion will turn to a confrontation with Hosea 1–3, a particularly problematic text for exegesis and interpretation. Feminist scholarship has long registered these early chapters as a rape text—and for good reason: in Hosea, female bodies are depicted as violently abused and tortured without mercy.[1] The passages that blatantly and cruelly call for the abusive punishment of both Gomer and female prostitution figures (2:3, 9–10) cannot be pardoned. YHWH, the God of the Hebrew Bible, does nothing to help Tamar: whereas he strikes dead Er and Onan, his engagement with Tamar is marked by inaction (Genesis 38). In 1 Kings 3 YHWH supposedly ordains Solomon with wisdom. But this divinely conferred wisdom serves to marginalise the two prostitutes. In Hosea 1–3, however, YHWH, together with his prophet, is directly involved in launching his violence at Gomer and the prostitution figures. Adopting the sex workers' standpoint compels us as readers to face up to the violence of both the biblical text and of interpretations by Christian interpreters. Both have propagated rape-supportive attitudes, which have targeted sex workers with particular force—and in the guise of divine love.

Let me provide a brief summary of Hosea 1–3, followed by an account of how Chinese biblical scholars treat this passage. Emphasis will be given to their treatment of Gomer and the prostitution figures. Following on from this comes an explanation of how I presented Hosea 1–3 to the sex workers during the reading exercise. After this, I will report the comments of the sex workers arising from the discussion. Again, these are marked by their standpoints. Let me say at the outset that the sex workers loathed this text, because they identified it as a text of danger and death.

At the same time, they took heed from it, sensing a note of caution for their own survival.

5.1 Gomer and the female prostitution figures in Hosea 1–3

In Hosea 1:1–9, Hosea receives his mission from YHWH to marry a woman of *zěnûnîm*—often translated as "prostitution" or "whoredom", so as to teach Israel that their disloyalty towards YHWH will amount to their own destruction. Hosea selects Gomer. They have three children and to each of them Hosea gives a name signifying YHWH's negative regard for Israel: Jezreel (a son) is named after the site of a notorious massacre; the name of Lo-Ruhamah (a daughter) means "no mercy"; and the name Lo-Ammi (for another son) means "not my people". Hosea 1:10–11 presents a brief message of hope for the future of Israel, reversing the effect of the negative names of the three children.

From Hosea 2 to 3, the language shifts, interchanging between Gomer and the prostitution metaphors of Israel and also between Hosea and YHWH. Hosea 2:1–4 opens with a symbolic address to Israel, calling Israel by the names Ruhamah ("mercy") and Ammi ("my people"), and charging the name holders to sue Gomer, their mother, as if in court. Their mother is stripped, exposing her nakedness and judgement is pronounced not only on her, but also on the children. Hosea 2:5–13 details how Hosea intends to imprison her, because she wants to run away to her lovers. He will ensure that she will never find them and he will cease all provisions to her, so that she will die of thirst and hunger. He will expose her genitals to all her lovers and the public—and cause paralysis to her lovers so that they can only watch but not save her. He will cause all her labour to come to naught.

Hosea 2:14–23 changes in tone from wrath to sentimentality: YHWH will be nice to her in order that she will respond meekly and give him undivided attention. Then he will swear that she shall be his wife again forever.

Hosea 3:1–5 begins with Hosea being sent on another mission. YHWH commands Hosea to go love an adulteress to show that YHWH still loves Israel even though the latter has disowned him. So, Hosea buys a woman. The text does not explain how or why this woman seems to be enslaved and has to be redeemed with monies. Hosea imposes a ban on her having intercourse with anyone including himself for many days. This is to symbolise that Israel will be abandoned for many days without any ruler or the gods and religious rituals they had taken for granted. At the end of it, YHWH will redeem them.

5.2 Hong Kong Christian interpretations

In this section I shall first look at one well-known Chinese commentary by Samuel Tang and a local popular Bible study guide commonly used by laypersons for small-group Bible study, written by Patrick So. Both DDW2 and DDW3 also have short excerpts on Gomer, which will be quarried.

Hosea 1–3 is not easy to interpret because the text keeps jumping between literal and figurative speech. Consequently, interpreters try to draw boundaries between the two. Many theories have been proposed and attempts made to grasp the ancient Near Eastern background, particularly of Canaanite cultic practices, in order to help determine these boundaries. The debates are many and could distract readers from the primary aim of this project. It is important, therefore, to concentrate primarily on what the Chinese scholars and writers make of Gomer and the other prostitution figures in terms of their various roles as prostitute, wife and mother; and then to explore how these commentators explain and justify the punishments that YHWH threatens for the female characters.

5.2.1 Prostitute, wife and mother

For Christians, God's reputation is at stake here because the divine call to Hosea is for him to marry a prostitute. Tang takes the issue seriously in a literal sense and presents a concise outline of the arguments, weighing up which aspects are most at stake.[2] He prioritises the integrity of Hosea's prophecy and therefore rejects that Gomer's prostitution is metaphorical. In other words, Hosea's message of YHWH's love for apostate Israel must be closely matched with the reality of Hosea's marriage—namely, that Hosea, like YHWH, is badly hurt by his actually unfaithful wife. He says that conservative scholars could not accept and were so disturbed by this fact (i.e. that the prophet marries a prostitute) that they interpret *zĕnûnîm* ("prostitution", "whoredom") in 1:2 as figurative. Tang, followed by So and DDW3, subscribes to the claims of ancient Greek historian Herodotus (fifth century BCE) that ancient Near Eastern women, before they were married, practised fertility cult rites and offered their bodies to male passersby at the temple.[3] For followers of YHWH this would constitute defilement and prostitution. The commentators, then, argue that such practices existed in the background of Gomer's upbringing and turned her promiscuous.[4] For them, Hosea's message of YHWH's love for Israel is crucial to redeem the Israelites from such a degrading religion and culture. In one sense, these scholars and writers see Gomer primarily as a victim of circumstances. Nonetheless, she is tainted by her promiscuity *(zěnûnîm)*. Tang explains further that because *zěnûnîm* can also refer to spiritual shortcomings, or idolatries, Gomer must have been spiritually deficient as well.[5] Hence, she practised fertility rites, inclusive of cultic prostitution and idolatry, before her marriage and that explains why she is called a woman of *zěnûnîm* (i.e. in the plural, 1:2): because the word pertains *both* to physical and spiritual defilement.

Tang proposes reading 2:1–7 as a precursor to 3:1; this may explain how Gomer ends up in such a miserable state of slavery and as an unwanted "adulteress" in Hosea 3.[6] Tang argues that the woman in Hosea 3 is also Gomer although she is not named here.[7] His reasons are that if it were to refer to someone else, that would mean Hosea had divorced Gomer to marry another woman. Tang believes Hosea would not have divorced Gomer because the prophet's message is about YHWH's faithfulness to his covenant despite his "wife's" adulteries (that is, his people's unfaithfulness). So, if YHWH will not forego Israel, despite Israel's disloyalty, Hosea must bear his hurt and humiliation and keep his wife, regardless of her conduct. So, this passage refers to Gomer, who has apparently left Hosea and her children for a period of time, although the text does not say for how long.

The Chinese writers say many negative things about Hosea's wife and emphasise that Gomer must be held accountable for her behaviour. They draw attention to her being the instigator of hurt and malignity, shaming her husband while gratifying her sexual appetites. For example, So calls on readers to ponder how they would feel if they found their spouse to be having multiple love affairs—how would one want to treat that spouse in return?[8] DDW2 also calls Gomer a spoilt and selfish lover and a sex addict, someone whom only God can deliver.[9] DDW2 also expresses sympathy for Hosea and for YHWH, emphasising the male figures' status as cuckolded husbands and victims of unrequited love. Both are credited with feelings of deep devastation and lauded as devoted husbands. The contrast in attitudes to male versus female characters is stark. Females are incorrigible, faithless and shameful; males are loving to the point of salvific devotion. For these Chinese commentators, Gomer has utterly failed as a wife and a mother. She is a stain on her husband and her children.

Tang holds that the three children are Hosea's and that Gomer wandered into her prostituting ways after giving birth to them.[10] He also posits that the children's names were originally positive ones but that Hosea altered them to signify Gomer's prostituting and its consequences. Tang admits that the name of the first-born, Jezreel, could hint that he did not belong to Hosea, and might be an outcome of her prostitution at the fertility rituals.[11] Tang also imagines that Gomer must have taught her children to follow the same fertility cult rites.[12] The notion that Gomer is fertile *after* practising such rites may have further encouraged her idolatrous worship of other gods. This way of interpretation (i.e. that one or more of Gomer's children was conceived through prostitution) could reinforce 1:2, according to which Hosea has "children of whoredom". He explains that society looks to one's parents to determine one's destiny.[13] Gomer's prostitution, whether she was a prostitute before, during, or after conceiving children, brings stigma to her children as well. Tang also interprets that it is up to Hosea to "sanctify" this family.

5.2.2 Justifications for punishment

For these Chinese writers, Gomer is the problem that needs fixing in this relationship. They keep reiterating her depravity and stressing their abhorrence of her behaviour. And this transpires in the assessment that Gomer deserves the extreme and violent punishment and discipline she receives.

As mentioned earlier, So has caricatured Gomer as a sex addict. Seemingly, she is utterly mired in her addiction and brings profound damage to her family.[14] Hosea has to summon their children to plead with their mother to "remove the prostitution from her face; and her adulteries from between her breasts" (2:2). If she does not comply, Hosea will strip her naked and expose her publicly. So, following Tang, explains that this alludes to a custom whereby at a wedding, the groom presents his bride with a new robe. If a wife is later found to have committed adultery (i.e. if she was not a virgin at the point of marriage or if she had sexual relations with a man other than her husband after marriage), then the robe is publicly stripped from her to humiliate her.[15] The metaphor of Gomer as a "parched land" also symbolises that Hosea will not provide for her anymore. Tang explains that the withdrawal of provisions is extended to the children as well, because they are implicated in her prostitution. Tang does not explain why this is the case. So, however, explains that since the children were the result of Gomer's prostitutions, Hosea is under no obligation to raise or provide for them: both Gomer and the children deserve their punishment. For Hosea to have accepted them at any point was generous on his part.

Tang moves between Hosea and YHWH interchangeably, as well as between Gomer and Israel, when explaining Hosea 2–3. He interprets the depictions of punishments as Hosea/YHWH's unsuccessful attempts to "correct" Gomer/Israel before ongoing prostitution becomes worse.[16] He summarises Hosea 2 as follows: Hosea/YHWH is determined not to divorce Gomer/Israel, and that is why a "court-hearing" is set up with the children as witnesses.[17] The husband figure attempts to show the wife figure what is wrong so that she may willingly repent and return to him. However, this plan fails. Tang defends Hosea/YHWH, claiming that he has only good intentions for her: namely, to correct her wrongs. Tang therefore thinks Hosea 2 is a failed attempt to restore Gomer. She is "enslaved" and an "adulteress" requiring redemption.[18] Apparently, she has to become debased to the state of enslavement before she can be redeemed. Tang interprets all the punishments meted out by the male figures as demonstrating what true love is: it is not cheap, rather, it is tough and requires discipline.

So's comments on Hosea 2–3 keep emphasising that Gomer and Israel must both repent, since not to do so is to forego all blessings.[19] It seems that YHWH is attempting to let Gomer/Israel realise this by withdrawing all provisions and removing all festivities. So then explains that humans learn best when they are made to undergo difficulties.[20] Hence, this is how Hosea/YHWH makes Gomer/Israel learn to rectify bad behaviours.

Both Tang and So interpret Hosea 3 as a demonstration and epitome of Hosea/YHWH's great love. So also makes an allusion here to God's incomparable love shown to Christians in the image of Jesus suffering on the cross. Like Tang, he stresses that love can require discipline.[21] There are several reasons for the enforced "many days" of isolation: to allow Gomer to reflect on and repent of her actions, to ensure that she is completely cut off from her lovers, and to establish whether she is pregnant by one of them. So explains that this enforced isolation is similar to the extended exile Israel must undergo: only when deprived of land, with Israel's monarch deposed and the temple of Jerusalem destroyed, will the people learn who their God really is. So goes on to preach that similarly, if anyone refuses to repent of their bad behaviour and habits, they will be deserted; left alone. Thus, it is important for everyone to repent and live righteously, so as not to procure severe punishment.

In summary, whatever Hosea and YHWH do and say about Gomer and Israel, it is all out of love and justified. These husbands are righteously angry and frustrated by their wives' incorrigible promiscuity. Wrongdoing, moreover, has consequences for others: hence, Gomer's children are judged along with their mother. The Chinese writers emphasise that the husbands could have merely abandoned their wives and children, but that this passage highlights their generosity extended to a defiled, undeserving and ungrateful mother and children. The punishments secure what is depicted as a happy ending: Gomer will be restored to the marital relationship. The punishments are necessary steps to discipline her and her children so that she can come to complete repentance.

These writers champion the following notion: true love involves tough discipline and Gomer needs it because she has become uncontrollable!

5.3 Sex workers' standpoints

As Hosea 1–3 portrays female characters in rather complex ways, I will outline here how I presented this passage to the sex workers.

The reading exercise began with a brief presentation about the three Hosea chapters. I explained that the term *'ēšet zĕnûnîm* (literally, "woman/wife of prostitutions") in biblical Hebrew uses a plural form, which might simply refer to something abstract. Recently, scholars have taken the expression to mean "a wife of promiscuity", to encapsulate a number of possibilities: a woman who *is* a prostitute, a woman who is *acting like* a prostitute, a promiscuous wife, and a woman who worships other gods beside, or instead of, YHWH.[22] Then, I explained the prophetic strategy of behaving strangely in order to act out and convey what God is communicating. Often what looks peculiar is symbolic of something that will or could happen in the future. Prophetic texts often use bizarre language or metaphors to shock the audience, or perhaps to make the audience ponder the message. The vicious descriptions in Hosea 2 and 3 sometimes blur the boundaries between what is described (i.e. the brutal treatment of a woman) and what this description signifies (i.e. the various types of punishment that will or could befall Israel in times to come).[23]

The passages were divided into three parts: Hosea 1 (Gomer's marriage to Hosea and the significance of their children's names); Hosea 2 (Hosea calls on the children to accuse Gomer, their mother; later Hosea/YHWH punishes Gomer and/or the female prostitution figures); Hosea 3 (an adulteress/prostitution figure/Gomer is sold as a slave and Hosea/YHWH buys her so as to take her as their wife). In the pause after reading each part we addressed any of the sex workers' questions. I also asked questions to see how they might respond. Most of the time, however, there was no need to raise a question or fill a silence, because the sex workers responded to the text spontaneously and, especially with Hosea 2 and 3, with fury.

For the purpose here, the sex workers' opinions and conclusions relating to three topics will be provided: 1) the problem of Hosea/YHWH condoning rape culture; 2) the victimization of Gomer and the female prostitution figures; and 3) the problem of the female prostitution metaphor. Each section was designed to highlight a discrete point but they all inevitably overlapped. Thus, the first sub-section cannot be appreciated fully until the sex workers' standpoints dealt with in the other two sub-sections are also grasped.

5.3.1 *The problem of Hosea/YHWH condoning rape culture*

The sex workers were disgusted with Hosea 2. They were appalled by the description of Hosea stripping Gomer naked in front of her children (2:3) and in front of all her "lovers" and the public (2:9–10). Most of them could not believe this passage was from the Bible. They were not appeased by the explanation that the removal of clothes reversed the symbolic action of the bridegroom giving a robe, or putting a robe on, his bride on their wedding, as the local commentaries explained. They argued if this were so, then Hosea could just remove Gomer's outer cloak to symbolise the end of their marriage, but he need not expose her nakedness. The public stripping is gratuitous and malicious, to the point of inviting rape in public and even letting the woman's children watch—thereby humiliating and traumatising both mother and children. Gomer's lovers/clients might also be humiliated and distressed because they could not save her. The sex workers saw this as a cruel and vengeful action on Hosea's part, saying to the rest of the world: since I cannot own her completely, let her die in utter humiliation and shame! And no one can save her from me, except me! Hosea, they said, is acting like a psychotic control freak.

What also upset the sex workers is that this punishment is sanctioned in the Bible, and meted out to Gomer, who is possibly, like them, a female sex worker. They talked about male potency: that the men controlled women's sexuality to the extent that they could justify their act of stripping women naked and possibly even raping them as though this were an acceptable punishment for sex workers, or any women deemed promiscuous. The sex workers were indignant that even if Gomer did indeed do something wrong against her husband, then this was not the way to punish her. Punishing someone should mean helping them to correct their wrongs. The punishment here is not corrective but destructive, crushing Gomer's personhood, self-respect and humanity. To the sex workers, this text is a rape text disguised with religious jargon and a text targeting sex workers for punishment on account of their profession.

Among biblical scholars, the punishment of Gomer is treated in a number of different ways. Gale Yee explains Hosea's punishment of Gomer in Hosea 2 as YHWH seeking the full measure of repayment for his loss.[24] That is, Hosea's revenge relates to the damage done to him on account of his wife's adulteries, which constitute a betrayal of their marriage. But alongside this human layer, the language of Gomer's body resembling "parched land" clearly equates her with the land of Israel. In the section under "Reflection", Yee warns against physical abusiveness, including when it comes in the guise of love.

Like Yee, James Mays also considers Gomer to be a real figure but he nonetheless reads the whole episode as primarily an allegory about relations between YHWH and Israel. He interprets the clothing as a symbol of a husband's provision for his spouse, and the stripping away of her clothing as the removal of his support.[25] In terms of how this metaphor functions, he understands Gomer's naked and starved body (v.3) to make the parched land more evocative. As for v.10, he simply asserts that the purpose of punishing Gomer is to urge her to cease her adulteries completely. Gomer is compelled to change or to suffer the consequences.

Francis Landy, however, rather like the sex workers, regards the punishment of public stripping as "pornographic" and as an invitation to "gang-rape".[26] Indeed, Yvonne Sherwood, too, laments that the text justifies male rape while blaming it on unfaithful women.[27]

5.3.2 The victimization of Gomer and the female prostitution figures

As the reading progressed, the sex workers began to formulate how in their view the biblical author seems to be creating a trap to victimise Gomer and the prostitution figures.

The sex workers' reaction to the first part of the reading (Hos 1:1–2:3) was to point out that they find Hosea and his God extremely problematic. They wondered, like some biblical interpreters did too: why does this God allow his prophet, Hosea, to marry a prostitute? Is it that the divine/religious "good" outshines the secular or profane/sexual "bad"?[28] One sex worker speculated that Hosea must have seen and fallen in love with Gomer early on and sought some excuse to marry her. Since he was a prophet, his action could best be excused by saying it was God who instructed him! Citing my earlier explanation that prophets do strange things to convey YHWH's message, she said that being a prophet had this advantage. Interestingly, A. Allwohn says something similar about the marriage of Hosea, seeing it "as an excuse for following his own sensual imagination".[29]

Next, the majority of the sex workers took issue with how Hosea named the children. They found that calling the children "children of harlotries" is not only an act of stigmatising but also of disowning them and indicative of a nasty transference of hatred from their mother to them. The sex workers reported that as mothers, they would have fought tooth and nail against such pejorative names. They said a good name is very important. So, even if the undisclosed intention was to reverse these negative names in the future when Israel was restored, that still means the poor children would have to carry these negative names until such time. A few believed that Hosea could only make these claims in his writing.

That is, in real life, the children would have lived with names Gomer gave them. (I had told the sex workers earlier that the Bible mentions mothers naming their children.)

Many commentators become caught up in explaining the significance of the children's names and argue, sometimes, that God predetermined their names.[30] Few considered the effects of such names on the children, or on the family as a whole. Landy comes close, imagining what names Gomer actually called her children.[31] If, as Sherwood argues, Gomer really was a shameless miscreant and Hosea a silenced and docile sufferer,[32] would she not—echoing the sex workers' standpoints—have fought for her children to have auspicious names? Then again, if either she or Hosea or God were depraved or abusive, might giving them such names affirm this perversity?

The sex workers, however, were more concerned with the welfare of the children than with the rights of the mother to name them. In their view, since Hosea did so poorly with the names, he should not have any part in their upbringing. One crucial point for me was that the sex workers identified that the names stigmatised Gomer *and* her children. The names carried deep impact for them, communicating that mother *and* children did not deserve mercy, only punishment. This pitches the children against their mother, to blame her and arouse hatred against her. This was, for the sex workers, Hosea's first victimization of Gomer: stigmatising children and setting them against their mother.

The sex workers did not take Hosea 2:14–23 and 3:1–5 to constitute a message of hope for Gomer or the prostitution figures. They shuddered when they went through the verses on how Hosea/YHWH intended to woo and restore the female figures to being wives again. They cringed and gasped in fear when hearing how the husband would isolate her from civilization, so that she only had him. The sex workers protested this is illegal imprisonment by a man clearly of unsound mind.[33]

They pointed out that throughout the story the husband figures were obviously jealous, overly possessive, physically abusive and sadistic. Under such circumstances, they said, they would rather die than return to this mentally disturbed husband. In the same breath, however, they also lamented that mothers so often return to their abusive husbands because of their children. They insisted: mothers must protect their children from their father. They also said that as soon as one's children are grown up and have become independent, then, and then only, should a woman leave her husband. The sex workers believed this was Gomer's story, too; that Gomer agreed to return solely because she could not leave her children in the care of this psychotic father. He would abuse them more severely if she were not around to manage his violent behaviour.

They explained that, as long as his attention was on his wife—venting his rage on her—he would not have energy left to attack the children. So, she alone must endure all the inhumane torture. She was compelled to keep silent and be imprisoned. Some of the sex workers admitted that they would have chosen the same route as Gomer. They all felt sorry for Gomer/the prostitution figures for being forced to buckle under dreadful conditions, returning to her husband and to her abusive marriage.

The sex workers also thought that the actions of the husband figures indicate that they need to possess women completely. These husbands seemed to believe that by imprisoning women, barring them from any interaction with the outside world, they could "rehabilitate" them and prevent them from running away again. They argued that the strategy of depriving a woman to the point of near-death with hunger and thirst and then suddenly making an about-turn to revive her, is indicative of severe mental illness. The sex workers were enraged and called Hosea/YHWH "mad" and someone who could not comprehend what mutual love and respect in a relationship were. They also seemed conflicted with respect to the deity's purpose and questioned why YHWH wanted to be associated with this prophet? Should this YHWH not rather heal and try to rehabilitate the prophet? The sex workers found it hard to accept that the two male figures are on the same side against the female characters. One even commented: if God's love, which Christians preach about, amounts to this, it is best not to have any part of it! Apparently, the Chinese Christian writers' insistence that these texts amplify God's love is not compelling for the sex workers.

One of the sex workers disagreed with the statements the others made concerning women's decision to return to abusive men because of the children. She said she would have turned to Hosea and told him: "YHWH just made me a prophetess and he wants me to kill you, because you are more wicked than all of Israel!" She asked, why should so many people suffer because of this wicked man, Hosea? She would *not* allow anyone to harm her in this way and would rather lose her life to fight for freedom. To submit to his torture also forces the children to submit to such oppressive forces. She said if women would not protest against such wicked threats on their lives, then the children would not learn to fight for what is right and just. In this way, cycles of abuse continue. She regretted that that is how abusive men keep oppressing women and that Hosea had used the strategy of disowning his children and acting terribly until Gomer submitted to him.

The sex workers' standpoints have identified reasons for the victimization of Gomer/the prostitution figures. They have also determined that children are their mothers' weak spot and that abusers often use children to threaten mothers, including mothers who are sex workers.

Conventional commentaries, like those outlined earlier, treat these passages as descriptions of the restoration of the female figures. They assert that the punishments are justified, for they are commensurate with the misdeeds of Gomer and the prostitution figures. Moreover, they regard Hosea in positive terms, as a forgiving husband, who, despite his harsh discipline, still wants Gomer back. He is willing to go to extremes to show how much he loves her and to restore her. However, Landy and Sherwood refuse to accept such interpretations of these passages.[34] Thinking along similar lines as the sex workers, they perceive an obsessive husband figure, filled with jealousy, who is sadistic in his punishment. Landy goes so far as to say that even Hosea's reconciliation programmes are deceptive, demonstrating only the outworking of hyper-masculinity for the purpose of controlling and subverting female sexuality. The sex workers' reading contributes to the reality of the terror of being dominated by violent men. They fervently resist the notion that violent male control can be justified or redemptive. The sex workers' reactions to these texts shows that they understand and that they have seen victimization and violence up close. Some expressed the urge in them to resist and fight back.

5.3.3 *The problem of the female prostitution metaphors*

At the end of the reading exercise, I reminded the sex workers of what scholars think the meanings of *zĕnûnîm* could be. I also mentioned that there were scholars who rejected the interpretation that Gomer was an actual prostitute, and that she might or might not be promiscuous, that perhaps she was above all or only idolatrous. So, I asked them if they think the term "prostituting", employed as a figure of speech for worshipping other gods besides or instead of YHWH, is an effective one. One answered using a Chinese idiom that this use of language is 殺雞儆猴. This idiom literally means, "to kill the chicken to warn monkeys", with the "monkeys" referring to "others". There is a double entendre here: in Chinese, "chicken" also refers to a sex worker. What she was saying is that this Hebrew usage has "killed" the prostitute/s in order to warn other people not to follow in her footsteps. The sex worker said this with exasperation and regret. She could not believe that the Bible contains a text where God condones the violent punishment of a prostitute and the endangerment of her children, depicting this as no more than an object lesson.

Another sex worker pointed out that this metaphor is a very poor one that is out of touch with reality: for in real life, it is not generally, in her experience, the woman who is unfaithful in the marriage but the man. The others concurred. I explained to them that "adultery" in the Bible is understood in terms of a recalcitrant married or betrothed *woman*. As long as a married man is not sleeping with any married or betrothed women, what he does is not considered to be adultery. Married women, however, cannot have sexual relations with *any* man, married or otherwise. I also added that this is to protect a man's patrilineal inheritance. The sex workers were indignant. Many of them commented that that kind of double standard is how men justify their own unfaithfulness to their wives, shifting blame onto women and especially onto sex workers. They expressed disdain at the unfair treatment in such cases and felt sorry for the women in the biblical period. All of them insisted that unfaithfulness is primarily a male problem, rather than a female one. They insisted that sex work is a profession that exists because of this male tendency. Then, one of them gave her considered opinion that since this definition of adultery is no longer relevant in today's world then the metaphor should be abandoned completely.

Further to the above point, two of them reasoned as follows: if the purpose of this metaphor is to persuade Israel to remain faithful to their God YHWH and not go to worship other gods, then the metaphor should personify a male, not a female. They said this because society in the biblical period was distinctly patriarchal in nature and males fulfilled the roles in the priesthood and enforced the laws; hence, it must follow that the offenders, too, would be mostly male, not female. It is pointless, they continued, to depict male transgression as an adulteress and a female prostitution figure, because men would not readily identify with such figures. Instead, males would identify with Hosea and with the masculine deity YHWH, both of whom did the punishing.

Another sex worker added that this twisted logic, according to which men missed the point of the metaphor that inculcated Israel to stop sinning, and instead identified with YHWH and with his prophet, is probably why Christians have become so judgemental of sex workers and why they consider it their right to look down on and to punish sex workers. Generally, the women agreed that this metaphor becomes an excuse to treat women and wives badly, because the metaphor casts women as naturally and uncontrollably promiscuous. One sex worker decided that the biblical author had "got it wrong": that YHWH should be on the side of the female characters who suffered pain and injustice but continued to be compassionate. Instead, Hosea was the recalcitrant culprit who deserved both punishment and mercy. She deemed the prophet not intelligent enough to produce this more faithful message and accused him of completely misrepresenting the genuine message of YHWH!

Interestingly, the last sex worker's standpoint is somewhat similar to the view of feminist commentator Fokkelien van Dijk-Hemmes, who argues that the metaphor for Israel's injustice and apostasy should be a rapist, and not an adulteress or prostitute.[35] In addition, other feminist scholars, such as Susanne Scholz, Renita Weems and Gale Yee, have also pointed out the inappropriateness of the gendering of this metaphor, because a male audience would identify more readily with Hosea's/YHWH's side, casting them as the righteous ones, justified in blaming and punishing women and sanctioning wife/spousal abuse.[36] Indeed, that interpretation is exactly what I identified in the exegetical works by the Chinese scholars and writers. Their interpretations led them not to consider those punishments as excessive but justified them all as "loving" and "necessary". Feminist scholars, however, while generally taking a view opposing this, nevertheless fall short in terms of acknowledging how these sacred texts represent a threat to sex workers. What needs to be emphasised is that Hosea 1–3 casts prostitutes as deserving targets of physical violence and rape. The horror of this was clear to the sex workers.

Secondly, more than half of the sex workers in the group could not accept the description that the male characters are the main providers and that Gomer would return to her husband because of a lack of sustenance (2:5-9; 12-13). They were also angry that Hosea forced Gomer to stop her work. They argued, this is not representative of reality. As far as the sex workers were concerned, they took up their profession "to put food on the table". They were the ones who secured the financial stability of their families—not their male spouses or partners. Those whose families had become impoverished had regularly been made vulnerable because men had abandoned the family, or because men had made poor investment decisions or because male partners had overspent or stolen from them. The point the sex workers were making is that they are the breadwinners and the ones who make financial decisions and look after children and parents. Therefore, these women interpret the text to say that Hosea/YHWH has forgotten Gomer's financial contribution to the family. They imagined that perhaps the family had regained financial stability after Gomer's hard work and that Hosea had become ungrateful and jealous of her achievements. Interestingly, Sherwood points out that Gomer's claim about what was hers was denied by the text,[37] and here the sex workers have argued the "how" and the "why".

A couple of the sex workers added that they had met clients who had offered to provide for them and urged them to discontinue their profession. But they had declined these offers because to agree would mean becoming these men's mistresses, which would compromise them. One reason for this is because their profession makes sexual services transactional and impersonal. But being a mistress would change this and implicate them in the client's own family relations. To become someone's mistress would involve and implicate them in jeopardising the client's family life. Dependence on one man might also make them reliant on his income or any inheritance, again with repercussions for the man's family. Moreover, "promises" made by men might not be reliable. Two sex workers believed that they should work hard now to secure their financial stability for their families and themselves while they could still work. They believed it would be better to remain independent rather than to entrust their future to a man who would control everything. Their experiences had informed them that men do not prove to be reliable providers.

Another sex worker pointed out that Gomer's story serves as a warning to working women. At the end of the day, the males would exert their control and claim that everything was theirs and blame every bad thing on their wives. Indeed, the Chinese commentator So actually interprets Hosea 2:1–4 as explaining that because the adulteries are completely Gomer's fault, Hosea is, therefore, exonerated from his duties as father and husband.[38] It seems that, for So, this way of thinking would exemplify how loving Hosea/YHWH is and how undeserving Gomer/Israel is. That interpretation actually reinforces irresponsible behaviour and lack of commitment to one's family on a father's behalf: as long as a husband can find fault with, or suspects, his wife, he is blameless and without responsibility—even for his children!

All the sex workers observed that the story indicates that Gomer is a successful prostitute, because the passage gives clues that she has a good client base (2:5, 11–13). This is not, however, depicted as a point in her favour. They maintained that it was wrong of Hosea to force her to quit by stopping her from seeing her clients. They protested that they would fight with Hosea if he were to do that to them! They concluded that the portrayal of Gomer deciding to "return to her husband" (2:7) is only valid in the imagination of this jealous Hosea. Gomer did not need Hosea's provisions—she had been independent as a prostitute, so she would know how to survive without a husband! This is why they argued this story is full of errors and misrepresentations.

Moving on, I asked the sex workers if they would prefer that Gomer were a real prostitute (taking the text literally), or if her prostitution were only metaphorical? The answers they gave were more complex than a mere "yes" or "no". Unanimously, they opposed the inhumane way Gomer and the female prostitution figures were treated. They were convinced that the biblical author (they insisted on a male author) was simply taking out his anger on Gomer. They believed he was a woman-hater. They all avowed that they wished all the wicked things that Hosea proclaimed had not taken place. Therefore, on this premise, they wished that none of the female characters were real persons.

At the same time, two sex workers expressed their preference that Gomer was a real prostitute. This was because they thought it important to have representatives of their profession in the Bible, or other sacred texts. They believed that the story of Gomer, in some ways, depicted the real sufferings of sex workers who are abused by their husbands. It is a negative story indeed and, at the same time, the sex workers can use it as a warning against evil men and/or husbands. In other words, they chose to read the text as a validation of their existence and as a warning—though not a warning in the sense that the biblical author intended, but from a female perspective, of warning other women against male control and brutality.

There were a few disagreements among the women because the texts found in a sacred book were seemingly justifying the torture of sex workers. This meant that the religion sanctions the marginalization and punishment of sex workers. They felt that negative stories of abused sex workers are already plentiful enough to use as warnings, so they did not wish to find one in the Bible, too. The sex worker who took the first opinion felt that it is important that there are stories about sex workers in the Bible, regardless if the stories are good ones or bad ones. To her, this is the reality of life—some have good lives and others bad ones. Even with the bad ones, there will be some believers who will try to verify these texts with sex workers' perspectives. Here she pointed at me, stressing what I am trying to do through these reading exercises. She felt that in that way, believers can become more educated and their opinions will change. The Bible for her, for all its awful stories, offers opportunities for learning and for understanding others' insights. In the end the sex workers declined to indicate their preference either way. They were indecisive on the point whether the story depicted a real or metaphorical prostitute and whether the story had potential for positive impact.

5.4 Chapter summary

In this chapter, the sex workers' standpoints challenged the conventional interpretation of Hosea 1–3 where Hosea/YHWH is the forgiving lover and husband to a recalcitrant, promiscuous Gomer/prostitution figures. The sex workers' standpoints showed how the biblical text's use of language and cast of characters can become dangerous to the livelihood and survival of sex workers. Hosea 1–3 is a rape text sanctioning rape, physical and psychological torture against sex workers. From the sex workers' perspective, this text denies them any personhood, or rights to protect themselves and their children from psychotic husbands. They felt horrified by the violence of the text and offended in terms of their dignity as mothers, their financial capabilities and economic independence, and their ability to stand up against abusive male figures.

The sex workers deem Hosea 1–3 to be troubling and problematic because it is ineffective in its primary purpose—namely, to call Israel to account. Instead, it throws the bulk of the blame on women and on sex workers in particular. Unfairly, it also stigmatises sex workers' children. The text not only justifies violent punishment but sanctifies it. It has failed to present the reality of sex workers' lives, and it has failed utterly as an object lesson to teach religious faithfulness to Israel's God. The upshot is a diatribe about the author's misogyny, in the course of this, sanctioning and promoting rape culture.

Notes

1 E.g. Susanne Scholz, *Sacred Witness: Rape in the Hebrew Bible* (Minneapolis: Fortress Press, 2008), 17–18; 93–9; 179–208; Yvonne Sherwood, *The Prostitute and the Prophet: Hosea's Marriage in Literary-Theoretical Perspective* (Journal for the Study of the Old Testament Supplement Series 212; Sheffield: Sheffield Academic Press, 1996); Naomi Graetz, "God Is to Israel as Husband Is to Wife: The Metaphoric Battering of Hosea's Wife", in *A Feminist Companion to the Latter Prophets*, ed. Athalya Brenner (Sheffield: Sheffield Academic, 1995), 126–45; Renita J. Weems, *Battered Love: Marriage, Sex and Violence in the Hebrew Prophets* (Minneapolis, MN: Fortress Press, 1995).
2 Samuel Y.C. Tang, *Twelve Prophets (II) Hosea* (Tien Dao Bible Commentary; Hong Kong: Tien Dao, 1984), 13–15; 46–9.
3 Tang, 47, 69; So, 17. Tang cites W. Baumgartner, "Herodots babylonische und assyrische Nachrichten", *Archiv Orientální* 18 (1950): 69–109. The original source is Herodotus, *Histories* 1.199.
4 Tang, 15; Patrick W. C. So, *Hosea—Long Suffering Love* (4th printing; Life Messages Series; Hong Kong: Tien Dao Publishing, 2016), 17–18.
5 Tang, 48.
6 Tang, 93.
7 Tang, 90–3.
8 So, 17, 22.
9 So, 25–7; DDW2, 299.
10 Tang, 13.
11 Tang, 47–8.
12 Tang, 50.
13 Tang, 48–9.
14 So, 26–7.
15 So, 26; Tang, 67.
16 Tang, 70–82.

17 Tang, 81–2.
18 Tang, 89–94.
19 So, 26–7.
20 So, 28.
21 So, 35.
22 Phyllis Bird, "'To Play the Harlot': An Inquiry into an Old Testament Metaphor", in *Gender and Difference*, ed. Peggy L. Day (Minneapolis, MN: Fortress Press, 1999), 75–94. Gale Yee rejects the interpretation that Gomer is an actual prostitute; cf. Yee, *The Book of Hosea* in "The Twelve Prophets" (The New Interpreter's Bible, vol. VII; Nashville, TN: Abingdon, 1996), 216. Also, Fokkelien van Dijk-Hemmes, "The Imagination of Power and the Power of Imagination: An Intertextual Analysis of Two Biblical Love Songs: The Song of Songs and Hosea 2", *Journal for the Study of the Old Testament* 44 (1989): 79.
23 I subscribe to the interpretations of Sharon Moughtin-Mumby, *Sexual and Marital Metaphors in Hosea, Jeremiah, Isaiah and Ezekiel* (Oxford Theological Monographs; Oxford: Oxford University Press, 2008). She has offered by far the most reliable analysis of the sexual and marital metaphor of Israel/Judah in current scholarship. Zeroing in on the passages in Hosea, she recommends that in order to be fair to the strangeness of prophetic speech, that is, the spontaneity and abruptness of ideas that are packed into the passages, one should differentiate the passages carefully, and decide whether they refer directly to Gomer, or to the sexual and marital metaphors of Israel/Judah. Nonetheless, in the reading exercise, it is difficult for the sex workers to draw the distinction so clearly since this is their first encounter with the text. Hence, while I try to keep the distinction, blurring in their treatment when they respond to the story occurs.
24 Yee, 224–5.
25 James Luther Mays, *Hosea: A Commentary* (Old Testament Library: Philadelphia, PA: SCM, 1969), 38–42.
26 Francis Landy, *Hosea* (Readings: A New Biblical Commentary; Sheffield: Sheffield Phoenix Press, 2011), 27–8.
27 Sherwood, 303–4.
28 Sherwood, 14.
29 Sherwood, 61. Sherwood outlines Allwohn's psychoanalytic interpretation of Hosea from: *Die Ehe des Propheten Hosea in psychoanalytischer Beleuchtung* (Beihefte zur Zeitschrift für die alttestamentliche Wissenschaft, 44; Berlin: deGruyter, 1926), 46–53.
30 Tang, 13. Others like Mays, 27–34 and even Yee, 217–19, are simply caught up in emphasising the reversal rather than saying more about the effect of this act on the children and Gomer.
31 Landy, 17.
32 Sherwood, 113–19; 244–5.
33 They actually used the English word "psycho" and sometimes its Cantonese equivalent, which can mean "madness".
34 Landy, 37–44; Sherwood, 137–8; etc.
35 van Dikk-Hemmes, 85.
36 Gale Yee, *Poor Banished Children of Eve: Woman as Evil in the Hebrew Bible* (Minneapolis, MN: Fortress Press, 2003); both Weems and Yee were cited in Scholz, 93–9.
37 Sherwood, 318–20.
38 So, 17–22.

6 Summary and conclusion

The primary purpose of this work has been to debunk certain rape myths: namely, that women with multiple sexual partners and especially sex workers are rapable, because they are immoral or in need of discipline, and less deserving of justice. Acceptance of such rape myths leads to appalling situations and injustices, whereby the rape of a sex worker is treated as somehow "acceptable" because sex is "what sex workers do" or "their job". Acceptance of these myths erases the heightened vulnerability of sex workers to the crime of rape. It also reduces the rape of a sex worker to "just sex". It denies sex workers the right to shout "rape!" when it happens and to demand justice and it exonerates perpetrators who commit violent crimes. These rape myths also entrench the widespread victimization and stigmatization of sex workers so that their opportunities to seek justice for any crime (not just rape but also theft or robbery) or to protect their welfare and that of their children are profoundly compromised. Rape myths, I argue, are disproportionately damaging and dangerous for sex workers.

Unfortunately, both the biblical representation and the conventional interpretations of the speech and actions of prostitutes further promote such myths, albeit perhaps unintentionally. It means that many Bible readers and Christians continue to absorb and perpetuate such myths. After all, the Bible is a sacred text and its words are widely held to be sanctioned by God. This applies also to the setting of Hong Kong where conservative commentaries of the Bible, uncritical of rape myths embedded in the biblical text, continue to dominate. While this cannot account for all the unjust treatment faced by sex workers in the present, in Hong Kong and elsewhere, the Bible and the rape myths it contains do have some influence and effect. Given the multiple challenges and injustices sex workers face—from police, courts of law, churches, the wider public—what can be done, should be done to defuse these texts. Confronting potentially toxic biblical texts and giving insight into sex workers' lives and perspectives is one strategy for embarking on this endeavour. That is what this book has strived to do.

After the introduction, summarising my purpose and the method of standpoint theory, I moved on, in Chapter 2, to describe the context of Hong Kong. This is in acknowledgement of the fact that rape culture looks different in different settings. I focused on a setting familiar to me where I was working at the time of data gathering. I introduced the laws governing rape in Hong Kong, as well as statistics on the crime of rape. I explained that in Hong Kong sex work is decriminalised, but laws limit where sex workers can conduct their services and how they can advertise them. Both are controversial and have a damaging impact on sex workers. Chapter 2 also mentioned some of the campaigns that bring awareness to the public about what rape culture is. For specific information on sex workers in Hong Kong, my information derived from the most reliable source: namely, the NGOs that provide holistic support and services to sex workers. I described these NGOs, again to provide a fuller sense of my context of focus.

Testimonies of and statistics about sex workers have been collated by NGOs and show the appalling prevalence of sex worker abuse by clients and police. The latter seem to target them specifically with some regularity. Moreover, Hong Kong police officers have received instructions to entrap sex workers and have "permission" for "body contact". This has made sex workers easy targets of police victimization and obstructed access to protection and legal aid. Law courts, too, as shown, have sometimes proven deficient avenues for sex workers to obtain justice.

The bulk of this book focused on three texts from the Hebrew Bible, each of which mentions prostitutes or prostitution: Genesis 38, 1 Kings 3:16–28, and Hosea 1–3. Each text is summarised, as are biblical interpretations, focusing particularly on commentaries accessible to Hong Kong Christians. These are then interfaced with standpoint interpretations by Hong Kong sex workers. My findings made the stigmatization and victimization of sex workers excruciatingly clear. They also indicated how rape myths target sex workers. The sex workers' standpoints provided new insights and expertise hitherto untapped by biblical scholars. The devastating potency of rape myths embedded in biblical texts is now incontrovertible.

Chapter 3 focuses on Genesis 38, the story of Tamar and Judah. From the sex workers' standpoints, this is a rape text. Onan's sexual act with Tamar infringes the stipulations of the levirate law and exploits Tamar, violating her body and the boundaries of her consent (38:9): *that is rape*. The sex workers drew that conclusion because they are familiar with and susceptible to abuse and rape, such as when clients refuse to pay or to keep to other mutually negotiated agreements for sexual transactions. Sex without consent is rape and when biblical interpreters fail to point out that what Onan does is rape, the seriousness of rape is downplayed. Rape culture thrives where rape is minimised, normalised or passed over. Consequently, being more alert to the toxic potential of this verse, and listening to the sex workers' insights, is important for resisting rape culture.

The sex workers also noted how Genesis 38 privileges Judah's needs and interests, while rendering Tamar's needs well-nigh invisible. The patriarch's intention to enforce the levirate law, his decision to send Tamar back to her father's house, to engage a prostitute, to pay for her services, and to punish Tamar for her pregnancy—all are justified and presented as reasonable. Tamar, on the other hand, has to accept both being handed to Onan and not being handed to Shelah. She is not consulted, nor are her wishes respected. Her needs are subjugated to those of Judah and only by taking great risk can she conceive children.

The sex workers rejected the portrayal of Judah's (male authoritarian) superiority that reinforced the power of those benefiting from a rape culture and argued that v.14 was the climax of the story. Hence, they argued, the story should *really* be Tamar's story, a story to claim empowerment: *she* recognised how she had been abused and mistreated by the family and *she* resolved to take full control of her own destiny. The sex workers were happy to claim Tamar's story as narrating aspects of their stories also. They were not ashamed of their decisions to take up sex work, because, like Tamar, they made that choice for their own survival and to secure a more promising future for their families.

The sex workers, again drawing on their own experiences, found the encounter of the prostitutes with Solomon in his court in 1 Kings 3:16–28 all too familiar. They noted that they and their children are also often stigmatised and victimised by police and law courts. Seeing matters from their standpoints revealed the element of fear they experienced when in the proximity of authority. They believed fear was the reason that one mother agreed to cleave the baby in half as Solomon bid, for they have come to expect violence from persons in authority. The sex workers are accustomed to being threatened, to fear of imprisonment, to precarious finances, to anxieties concerning their children and futures, and to abuse and violence from clients, police officers and legal organs. Out of fear, they often could not resist or physically fight back. The sex workers confirmed that the notion that "real" victims of rape will fight their attackers and then report the crime and assert their rights is a rape myth. While some rape victims might stand up to the ordeal of rape at every step, many others are immobilised by fear or, quite simply, resigned. Therefore, the sex workers firmly rejected the idea that this is a story of kindness and wisdom and of prostitutes' equality before the law. Ultimately, they decided, the story did not convey a positive portrayal of prostitutes but rather engrained the usual damaging stereotypes.

In Chapter 5, the sex workers' standpoints served to resist vociferously the rhetoric of punishment for Gomer and the prostitution figures of Hosea 1–3. The sex workers pointed to the humiliation and injustice of exposing the women's bodies in public and even in front of their children. This literary manoeuvre, even if it "only" constituted a metaphor, created an invitation to gang rape—whether in the mind or in actuality—and, they insisted, no human being deserved this, no matter what sins they might have committed. The sex workers were especially upset that the violent and voyeuristic punishment was proclaimed in the divine and/or prophetic voice. This, they argued, actually encouraged Christian males to behave in a similarly vitriolic and misogynistic way towards women *they perceived* to be promiscuous. Moreover, the passage extended vitriol also to the women's children and again, granted divinely sanctioned *carte blanche*. The sex workers recognised the danger of this.

Throughout the sex workers' engagement with the three texts, there is consistent demonstration of their considerable capacity for compassion and empathy, as well as for their high moral standards. Such a realization might surprise some readers, yet, it is clear to me and evident by what I report in this book. The view that sex workers are immoral and deserve their stigmatization is nothing other than prejudice. With the story of Tamar, for instance, the sex workers' assessment as to why Tamar does not seduce Judah sooner (i.e. because his wife is alive) speaks volumes about their sensitivity and respectfulness. Similarly, in the story about the two prostitutes coming before Solomon, they were upset that the Bible author and Solomon offer no respect to, or even mention, the dead child or the grief of his mother. As for the story of Gomer and the prostitution figures in Hosea 1–3, the sex workers demonstrated far more humane reactions than the majority of interpreters who insisted instead, against the textual evidence, on Hosea/YHWH's *love* for Gomer. Their personal standpoints informed the sex workers' abhorrence towards the physical and psychological bullying of the female figures.

The sex workers' standpoints on the three biblical texts have assuredly challenged conventional interpretations of these stories. These women have shown how and why the frequent tendency of biblical interpreters to take stories about prostitutes at face value, agreeing with the perspectives of the narrators, might lead them to fall short in terms of confronting deep-seated prejudices and stereotypes, including those reflecting rape culture.

Summary and conclusion

This work has tried to bring to readers' attention to first, how texts about prostitutes in the Bible tend to be interpreted, and second, how this can have lasting effects on how communities of faith perceive sex workers today. As the foregone chapters have shown, Hong Kong sex workers suffer at the hands of police and law courts. The treatment of prostitutes in biblical texts is also marked by threat and violence. In both settings this constitutes injustice. Christian readers and interpreters of the Bible have a moral responsibility to be cognizant of and sensitive to the vulnerability of sex workers. This work aims to convince Christians and biblical interpreters of the need to reflect and to ask probing questions: is interpretation of the prostitutes in the Bible a contributing factor to the stigmatization and victimization of sex workers in contemporary societies? Can uncritical interpretations promote rape culture and contribute to the harm of vulnerable communities, including sex workers? How can we make society more just, including for sex workers?

In conclusion, I would like to call to readers' minds the voice of protest of one of the sex workers cited in Chapter 5. Several others had resigned themselves to the fate of returning to their abusive husbands on account of their children. But this sex worker resisted. She protested that if a mother does not fight against her violent husband, then her children would not learn to fight for justice, or free themselves from oppression. In a similar way, I hope readers of this book will not just feel resigned to the pervasiveness of rape culture. Instead, I hope they will take a stand for transformation. This can begin with calling out discrimination against, and with educating others about the circumstances and challenges experienced by, sex workers. Perhaps, step by step, victims of rape and victims of rape culture will be believed, supported, granted justice and nurtured.

Selected bibliography

Action for REACH OUT. 2005. *A Survey on Hong Kong Police's Attitudes Towards Sex Workers*. Retrieved from: https://www.afro.org.hk/EN/pdf/ survey/survey_report_eng.pdf

Adorjan, Michael. 2019. "Perceptions of Policing and Security Among Hong Kong Migrant Sex Workers—A Research Note". *Asian Journal of Criminology* 14.2: 103–11.

Amnesty International. 2016. *Harmfully Isolated: Criminalizing Sex Work in Hong Kong*. London: Amnesty International.

Baumann, G. 2003. *Love and Violence: Marriage as Metaphor for the Relationship Between YHWH and Israel in the Prophetic Books*. Trans. L.M. Maloney. Collegeville, MN: Liturgical.

Bird, P. 1989. "The Harlot as Heroine: Narrative Art and Social Presupposition in Three Old Testament Texts". *Semeia* 46: 119–39.

Bird, P. 1997. "The End of the Male Cult Prostitute: A Literary-Historical and Sociological Analysis of Hebrew *qadesh-qedeshim*". *Supplements to Vetus Testamentum* 66: 37–80.

Claasens, Juliana M. 2012. "Resisting Dehumanization: Ruth, Tamar, and the Quest for Human Dignity". *The Catholic Biblical Quarterly* 74.4: 659–74.

Faraone, Christopher and Laura McClure, eds. 2006. *Prostitutes and Courtesans in the Ancient World*. Madison, WI: University of Wisconsin.

Friedman, Mordechai A. 1990. "Tamar, a Symbol of Life: The 'Killer Wife' Superstition in the Bible and Jewish Tradition". *Association for Jewish Studies* 15: 23–61. doi: 10.1017/S0364009400002804

Graetz, Naomi. 1995. "God Is to Israel as Husband Is to Wife: The Metaphoric Battering of Hosea's Wife". In *A Feminist Companion to the Latter Prophets*, edited by Athalya Brenner, 126–45. Sheffield: Sheffield Academic Press.

Gravett, Sandie. 2004. "Reading 'Rape' in the Hebrew Bible: A Consideration of the Language". *Journal for the Study of the Old Testament* 28.3: 279–99.

Harding, Sandra, ed. 2004. *The Feminist Standpoint Theory Reader: Intellectual and Political Controversies*. New York/London: Routledge.

Havea, Jione. 2003. *Elusions of Control: Biblical Law on the Words of Women*. Leiden: Brill.

Hornsby, T. 1999. "'Israel Has Become a Worthless Thing': Rereading Gomer in Hosea 1–3". *Journal for the Study of Old Testament* 82: 115–28.

Ipsen, A. 2009. *Sex Working and the Bible*. London/Oakville: Equinox.

Kao, Ernest. 2012. "More Sex Workers Report Abuse by Police, Survey Finds". *South China Morning Post*, 17 December. Retrieved from: www.scmp.com/news/hong-kong/article/1107100/more-sex-workers-report-being-abused-police.

Keefe, A. 2002. *Woman's Body and the Social Body in Hosea*. Journal for the Society of Old Testament Supplement Series 338. Gender, Culture, Theory 10. Sheffield: Sheffield Academic Press.

Laidler, Karen Joe, Carole Petersen and Robyn Emerton. 2007. "Bureaucratic Justice: The Incarceration of Mainland Chinese Women Working in Hong Kong's Sex Industry". *International Journal of Offender Therapy and Comparative Criminology* 51.1: 68–83.

Landy, Francis. 2011. *Hosea*. Readings: A New Biblical Commentary. Sheffield: Sheffield Phoenix Press.

Li, Jessica C.M. 2013. "Violence Against Chinese Female Sex Workers in Hong Kong: From Understanding to Prevention". *International Journal of Offender Therapy and Comparative Criminology* 57.5: 613–31.

Messina-Dysert, Gina. 2015. *Rape Culture and Spiritual Violence: Religion, Testimony and Visions of Healing*. London/New York: Routledge.

Moon, J. 2015. "Honor and Shame in Hosea's Marriages". *Journal for the Study of Old Testament* 39.3: 335–51.

Moughtin-Mumby, S. 2008. *Sexual and Marital Metaphors in Hosea, Jeremiah, Isaiah and Ezekiel*. Oxford: Oxford University Press.

Newsom, C.A. and Sharon Ringe, eds. 1992. *The Women's Bible Commentary*. Louisville, KY: Westminster/John Knox.

Ng, Vivien. 1987. "Ideology and Sexuality: Rape Laws in Qing China". *Journal of Asian Studies* 46.1: 57–72.

Schneider, T. 2008. *Mothers of Promise: Women in the Book of Genesis*. Ada, MI: Baker Academic Press.

Scholz, Susanne. 2008. *Sacred Witness: Rape in the Hebrew Bible*. Minneapolis, MN: Fortress Press.

Seow, Choon-Leong. 1999. *1 & 2 Kings*. The New Interpreter's Bible. Vol. 3. Nashville, TN: Abingdon.

Sherwood, A. 2006. "A Leader's Misleading and a Prostitute's Profession". *Journal for the Study of the Old Testament* 31.1: 43–61.

Sherwood, Y. 1996. *The Prostitute and the Prophet: Hosea's Marriage in Literary-Theoretical Perspective*. Journal for the Study of the Old Testament: Supplement Series 212. Sheffield: Sheffield Academic Press.

Weems, Renita J. 1995. *Battered Love: Marriage, Sex and Violence in the Hebrew Prophets*. Minneapolis, MN: Fortress Press.

Wong, W.C.W., E. Holroyd, et al. 2008. "'One Country, Two Systems': Socio Political Implications for Female Migrant Sex Workers in Hong Kong". *BMC International Health and Human Rights* 8: 13. doi: 10.1186/ 1472-698X-8-13

Biblical texts index

Hebrew Bible

1 Kings 65
1 Kings 1–11 64
1 Kings 3 68,
1 Kings 3:1 64
1 Kings 3–11 64
1 Kings 3–15 55
1 Kings 3:16–28 5, 8–10, 11n7, 54–5, 68, 87–8
1 Kings 3:16 56, 62–3
1 Kings 3:17 62
1 Kings 3:18 11n7
1 Kings 3:26b 60
1 Kings 3:28 64

2 Samuel 15:3 63

Deuteronomy 22:23–27 55
Deuteronomy 25:5–10 31, 34

Genesis 19 41, 50–1n28
Genesis 19:8 41, 50n28
Genesis 37 50n27
Genesis 38 8–10, 31, 49, 50n 27, 68, 87–8
Genesis 38:9 38, 49, 87
Genesis 38:11 33, 41
Genesis 38:14 33–4, 40, 42, 45–6, 49
Genesis 38:15 11n7
Genesis 38:16b–18 38
Genesis 38:18 33–4
Genesis 38:20–23 33, 35
Genesis 38:20–25 45
Genesis 38:24 41
Genesis 38:24–25 33, 35
Genesis 38:26 10, 38, 41, 45–6

Hosea 1 74
Hosea 1–3 8–10, 68, 87–8
Hosea 1:1–9 69
Hosea 1:1–2:3 76
Hosea 1:2 71–2
Hosea 1:10–11 69
Hosea 2 72–5
Hosea 2–3 69, 72–3
Hosea 2:1–4 69, 82
Hosea 2:1–7 71
Hosea 2:2 72
Hosea 2:3 68, 75–6
Hosea 2:5 82
Hosea 2:5–13 69
Hosea 2:5–9 81
Hosea 2:7 82
Hosea 2:9–10 68, 75
Hosea 2:10 76
Hosea 2:11–13 82
Hosea 2:12–13 81
Hosea 2:14–23 69, 77
Hosea 3 71–4
Hosea 3:1–5 69, 77
Hosea 3:1 71

Joshua 2:1; 6:17, 11n7, 22–23, 25
Judges 11:1, 16:1 11n7
Judges 19–21 41, 50–1n28
Judges 19:24 41, 50n28

New Testament

Romans 14:21 18

For Product Safety Concerns and Information please contact our EU
representative GPSR@taylorandfrancis.com
Taylor & Francis Verlag GmbH, Kaufingerstraße 24, 80331 München, Germany

www.ingramcontent.com/pod-product-compliance
Lightning Source LLC
Chambersburg PA
CBHW051758230426
43670CB00012B/2336

68, 70–1, 74–5, 77–80, 83, 89; as female prostitution figures 9, 68–9, 74, 76, 79–80, 83
feminist 4–7, 20, 68, 81

God/god/s 11n7, 18, 37, 47, 51n28, 56–7, 64, 68–74, 76–80, 84, 86
Gomer 9, 11n7, 68–79, 81–3, 85n22, 85n23, 85n30, 89

Harding, Sandra 6, 12n12, 12n13
Havea, Joine 46, 52n33
Hirah 31–3, 35, 38–9, 46–8
Hong Kong Christian Council 18–9, 28n22
Hosea (prophet) 69–83, 89
Hui, LK Sherry 2, 11n3, 23, 61
husbands 33–4, 48, 49n4, 50n28, 53–4, 62, 71–3, 75–9, 81–4, 90

immoral 13, 24, 58, 86, 89
indecent *see* assault
injustice 3–4, 7, 9, 21, 26, 42, 46, 61, 68, 80–1, 86, 89–90; *see also* justice
interpret 4, 10, 32, 35–6, 45–6, 48–9, 49n10, 56, 62, 64, 70, 72–3, 76, 81–2, 90; as interpreter/s 4, 5, 8, 70, 76, 88–90; *see also* biblical interpreters
interpretations 5, 7–10, 17, 31–2, 38–9, 42, 45–8, 51n31, 55, 57, 64–5, 66n5, 66n25, 68, 72, 79, 81–3, 85n22, 85n23, 85n29, 86–7, 89–90; *see also* biblical interpretation; Christian interpretation
Ipsen, Avaren 5, 7–8, 11n8, 11n9, 22, 29n40, 58, 59, 62–4, 66n28, 66n29

JJJ, Jei Jei Jai Association 2, 5, 8, 11n3, 22–3, 29n39, 61
Judah (person) 9–10, 31–49, 50n27, 50n31, 87–9; as a people/location 85n23
justice 3–4, 6, 20, 36–7, 51n28, 54–7, 59, 61–3, 65, 86–7, 90

Kwong, P. C. Andrew 32–6, 39–40, 45–7

Landy, Francis 76–7, 79
laws (general) 4, 17, 20, 38, 44, 57, 59, 65, 89; in the bible 5, 31, 33, 38,

Subjects and authors index   95

80, 87–9; Hittite Laws §193 34; of Hong Kong 5, 9–10, 20–1, 24–5, 61, 65, 68, 86–7, 90; Law (Torah) 34–6, 39–40; laws governing sex work 24–6, 30n48; rape laws 13–5, 17, 20, 38, 87; in U.S. 5, 17
levirate 31, 33–4, 40, 87–8
Li, Paul 56–7, 62

MacKinnon, Catherine A. 17, 27n14
marginalise/marginalised 6–7, 10, 47, 49, 62, 68
marginalization 6, 10, 45, 47, 64, 83
McClure, K. 6, 12n15
Midnight Blue 22
misogyny 20, 42, 84, 89
mothers/motherhood 11n7, 22, 26, 41, 54–8, 60, 62–3, 66n18, 69–77, 79, 84, 88–90; mother-in-law 42
Moughtin-Mumby, Sharon 85n23
murder 13, 23, 25–6

NGOs 2, 4, 9, 11n6, 13, 15, 18–9, 21–4, 26, 28n16, 87

one-roomed/one room 13, 25

patriarch 9, 41, 88
patriarchy 17, 46, 80
perpetrators (as rapists) 3–4, 9, 14, 19, 60, 65, 86; *see also* rapist
police 1, 4, 10, 11n6, 13, 15–16, 18–9, 21, 23–6, 29n37, 53–5, 58–62, 65, 66n21, 68, 86–8, 90; as Hong Kong Police 15, 25
promiscuous 4, 9, 70–1, 73–5, 79–80, 83, 89
prostitutes 3–5, 8–9, 11n7, 31–2, 34–6, 39–49, 53–65, 70–2, 74, 76, 79, 81–3, 85n22, 86–90; as cult/shrine/temple prostitute 32, 35, 37, 46–7, 52n36
prostitution 8–9, 11n7, 26, 41, 63, 68–72, 74, 76–80, 82–3, 87, 89; *see also* female prostitution figures
punish/punishment 4, 9, 13, 26, 36, 39, 41–2, 47, 51n28, 54, 68, 70, 72–7, 79–81, 83–4, 88–9

qdsh 10, 32–3, 35, 38–9, 46–9; as *qdshym* 35

RainLily 15, 18–19, 27n8, 28n16, n17
rape/raped 1–4, 9–10, 11n3, n5, 13–21, 25–6, 29n30, 38–44, 50n28, 54–5, 60–1, 65, 68, 75–6, 81, 84, 86–8, 90; gang rape 41, 51n28, 76, 89; male rape 14, 76; statistics in Hong Kong 15–16; *see also* laws of rape
rape culture 2–5, 8–10, 13, 16–21, 26, 31, 37–8, 41–2, 74–5, 84, 87–90; definition of 2
rape myths 3–4, 10, 13, 17–20, 54–5, 61, 65, 86–8
rape texts 10, 38, 49, 55, 68, 75, 84, 87
rapists 2, 16–8, 55, 81; *see also* perpetrators

Schneider, Tammi 45, 51n31
Scholz, Suzanne 81, 85n36
sex work 3, 5, 7, 9, 12n19, 13, 21–6, 43, 47, 53, 58–9, 64, 80, 87–8
sexist 44
sexual: content 15, 63; harassment 18–21, 49; minorities 15; needs 41; offences 13–14, 19, 21; violence 3–4, 18–21, 26, 29n30; *see also* crime
shame 7, 18, 35, 40, 71, 75
shameless 1, 77
Sherwood, Yvonne 76–7, 79, 81, 85n29
SlutWalk 13, 19–20, 26
So, W. C. Patrick 70–3, 82
Solomon 5, 9, 53–64, 68, 88–9
standpoint theory 5–9, 12n16, 87
standpoints 20, 26, 45, 48, 68, 87–9; of sex workers' 10, 31, 37, 48, 55, 57, 64–5, 68, 74, 77–8, 81, 83, 87–9
stigma 2, 4, 13, 17, 31, 39, 72, 76–7, 84, 88
stigmatization 4, 5, 8–10, 26, 31, 38, 47, 55, 65, 86–7, 89–90

Tamar 9–10, 11n7, 31–49, 50n27, 51n31, 52n36, 68, 87–9
Tang, Samuel 70–3
Teen's Key 22–3
temple prostitute *see* prostitute
threat 1, 4, 10, 14, 38, 43–4, 48–9, 53, 60–5, 70, 78–9, 81, 88, 90
Tsai, Rei Yi 56–8, 62–3

victim/victims 1–4, 9, 13–21, 26, 28n16, 39, 50n28, 54–5, 61, 65, 70–1, 88, 90; victim-blaming 17–21
victimization 4–5, 8–10, 26, 39, 74, 76–9, 86–7, 90
violence 2–5, 9–10, 11n6, 20–1, 25–6, 50n28, 54, 58–9, 61, 64–5, 68, 79, 81, 84, 88, 90; *see also* sexual violence

Weems, Renita 81, 85n36
Wenham, Gordon 45–6
whore/whoredom 42, 69, 70, 72
wife 31–2, 34, 36, 38, 41, 49n4, 50n27, 51n28, 63–4, 69–74, 77–8, 80–2, 89
woman/women 1, 3–4, 6–7, 11n7, 14, 17–20, 22–3, 29n30, 32–5, 37–42, 44–5, 47–8, 50–1n28, 54–60, 62–5, 69–71, 74–84, 86, 89; as womanhater 83

Yee, Gale 75–6, 81, 85n22, 85n30, 85n36
YHWH 11n7, 31, 33, 37, 39–40, 47, 50–1n28, 55, 68–83, 89

zēnûnîm 69–71, 74, 79
Zi Teng 4, 11n6, 13, 21–3, 30n45, 30n46, 60
znh 5, 11n7, 34–6, 39, 46